The Tale of Little Red Riding Hood

An Untraditional Pantomime

Simon Brett

A SAMUEL FRENCH ACTING EDITION

SAMUEL FRENCH

FOUNDED 1830

SAMUELFRENCH-LONDON.CO.UK
SAMUELFRENCH.COM

FOR AMATEUR PRODUCTION ENQUIRIES

UNITED KINGDOM AND WORLD EXCLUDING NORTH AMERICA

plays@SamuelFrench-London.co.uk

020 7255 4302/01

Each title is subject to availability from Samuel French,

depending upon country of performance.

THE TALE OF LITTLE RED RIDING HOOD

First performed at The Theatre, Chipping Norton, on December 7th, 1995, with the following cast:

Natasha Boronski, Little Red Riding Hood	Caroline Faber
Katerina, her mother	Mandy Holliday
Basil, her brother	Justin Fletcher
Boris, her other brother	David Kangas
The Wolf	Chris MacDonnell
The Fox	Jo-Anna Lee
Babushka, granny	Stirling Rodger
Ivan, a woodcutter	Stephen Fewell

Chorus:
Red Team: Ben Higgins, Grace Hudson-Evans, Alex Vulliamy, Joshua Clacy
Blue Team: Christopher Brooke-Hollidge, Louis Parkinson, Amy Boning, Jessica Hayes

Directed by **Patricia Doyle**
Produced by **Tamara Malcolm**
Sets by **Colin Winslow**
Lighting by **Stephen Rate**

Musicians:
Sarah Travis (Musical Director)
Ashley Stevens

CHARACTERS

(In order of appearance)

Natasha Boronski, Little Red Riding Hood
The Countess Katerina Boronski, Natasha's mother
Prince Basil Boronski, Natasha's brother
Prince Boris Boronski, Natasha's other brother
Wolf
Fox
Babushka, Natasha's grandmother
Ivan, woodcutter
Ducks, **Vampire Bats**, and **Villagers**

SYNOPSIS OF SCENES

ACT I

ACT II

MUSIC PLOT

Overture

ACT I

1.	**Winter's Ending, Spring is Coming**	Katerina, Natasha, Basil, Boris
2.	**Winter's Ending, Spring is Coming (Fox's Version)**	Fox
3.	**Why Won't the Young Leave the Old Folks Alone?**	Babushka
4.	**Fox's Speech**	Fox
4a.	**Fox's Speech (reprise)**	Fox
4b.	**Ivan's Magic Spell**	Ivan
5.	**Just a Little Snack**	Katerina, Natasha, Basil, Boris, Ivan
6.	**Unrequited Love Duet**	Ivan, Natasha
7.	**Keeping the Wolf From the Door**	Katerina
8.	**Duck Dance**	Instrumental
9.	**The One That Got Away**	Basil, Boris
10. & 10a.	**Underscore and So Alone**	Wolf, Fox, Natasha
10b.	**Unrequited Love Duet (reprise)**	Ivan
11.	**Knitting Song**	Babushka

Entr'acte

ACT II

12.	**Follow the Fox**	Fox
12a.	**Follow the Fox (reprise)**	Fox
13.	**Cossack Dance**	Boris, Basil, Wolf
14.	**Frozen Lake**	Ivan, Fox
15.	**Vampire Dance**	Fox
16.	**Interior Design**	Babushka, Katerina, Natasha, Boris, Basil
17.	**Tickling Song**	Babushka, Katerina, Natasha, Boris, Basil
18.	**Requited Love Duet**	Ivan, Natasha
19.	**Winter's Ending, Spring is Coming**	All
20.	**Finale**	All
21.	**Calls and Interior Design (reprise)**	Company

The piano vocal score and violin part is available on hire from Samuel French Ltd.

PRODUCTION NOTES

Casting

In the original production **Ivan** was played by a man, but there is no reason why the role may not be played by a girl in "Principal Boy" tradition. Ivan's songs may easily be adapted for a female voice.

Similarly, the **Fox** was played by a woman originally, but could be played by a man.

When Babushka enters in her bed in Scene 5 of Act I and in subsequent scenes, she is wheeling herself on with her legs unseen under trailing drapes and a false body propped up in front of her on the bed.

When Boris steps on the block of ice in Scene 9 of Act I, the ice is in fact a cunningly disguised skateboard with hidden wheels.

When in Scene 2 of Act II the front of the bed opens to swallow Natasha, the mechanics can be manipulated under the bedclothes by the Wolf.

Other plays by Simon Brett
published by Samuel French Ltd

Mr Quigley's Revenge
Murder in Play
Silhouette

ACT I

SCENE 1

Overture

The Boronskis' sitting-room

The room is in semi-darkness. Hot coals glow through the grille of the stove, on top of which Boris is asleep. Steam rises comfortingly from the samovar. A door is suddenly opened on one side of the stage, spreading sunlight across the room. Birdsong is heard; this melts into music, which underscores the action until it leads into the opening song

Natasha, wearing her warm knitted red riding hood, enters excitedly through the door, carrying a bunch of snowdrops. Casting off her red riding hood on to the floor, she hurries across to a window and throws back the shutters, letting in more sunlight

Natasha (*calling offstage*) Mummy! Mummy! It's nearly spring!

Katerina enters

Katerina What, Natasha?
Natasha (*showing the flowers*) Look what I found! The first snowdrops!
Katerina Oh, thank goodness, the winter's almost over. (*She calls offstage*) Boris! Basil!

Basil enters

Basil What gives, Mummy?
Katerina Spring, Basil, spring! And where's Boris?
Basil Where do you think? (*He reaches up to the top of the stove to pull his brother's leg*) Boris, shake a leg!
Boris (*blearily*) Errh?
Basil (*pulling him down*) Wake up!
Natasha It's nearly spring!

Boris shakes the sleep out of his head, as the four Boronskis break into song

No. 1: Winter's Ending, Spring is Coming

All   We're the Boronskis, noble and rich
Thanks to our farmworkers' labours.
We live in a house which is gracious and which
Is bigger than those of our neighbours.
What we have is so much finer—
All our silverware and china—
We look down on the rest like anything,
'Cos our furniture's much plusher
Life is good to us in Russia—
And it won't be long until the spring.

Winter's ending, spring is coming,
Soon the ice will start to thaw
Green will show
Up through the snow,
And the melting water pour
Down the gutters.
Open shutters
Will let sunshine through your door.

One by one, the Boronskis step forward and address the audience

Katerina   My name is Katerina Boronski—or
The Countess Boronski to you.
Natasha   My name is Natasha Boronski and
I am a thoroughbred too.
Basil   My name is Prince Basil Boronski and
I'm clever at everything.
Boris   (*yawning*) My name is Prince Boris Boronski and
I keep falling... (*He yawns again and falls asleep*)
Katerina (*nudging him*)   Wake up and sing!

All   Winter's ending, spring is coming,
Soon the ice will start to thaw
Green will show
Up through the snow,
And the melting water pour
Down the gutters.
Open shutters
Will let sunshine through your door.

At the end of the song, the family group breaks up. Boris climbs surreptitiously back to his haven on top of the stove and snuggles down

Katerina If it's nearly spring, it means that Sergei, your father, will soon be back from Moscow.

Natasha Hooray! He's going to bring me a new coat—the very latest Paris fashion—and I can stop wearing that horrid red riding hood.

Katerina Now come on, Natasha, your grandmother knitted that for you.

Natasha You don't need to remind me. (*She picks the coat up off the floor*) And what kind of girl would ever be seen dead in anything knitted by her grandmother?

Natasha exits, dragging her red riding hood ungraciously

Basil I say, Mummy, if Daddy's about to come back from Moscow, Boris and me'd better get on with doing all the things we promised we'd do while he was away. Hadn't we, Boris?

There is no response. Boris is once again asleep. Basil looks around for him

Boris?

Katerina What did you promise your father you'd do, Basil?

Basil Oh, you know, the usual stuff—go round the estate and distribute Christmas presents to all the serfs.

Katerina But it's weeks after Christmas.

Basil I know, but with all presents, it's the thought that counts.

Katerina So?

Basil Well, I thought about giving the serfs their presents lots of times. I thought about it on Christmas Day. Just haven't got round to actually doing it yet, that's all.

Katerina Well, you go and do it straight away. (*On her way out*) You don't want to make your father angry, do you?

Katerina exits

Basil (*heartfelt*) No, no, I jolly well don't. (*Finally he sees Boris on top of the stove*) Come on, Boris! We've got work to do!

Boris (*blearily*) Work? What a disgusting idea! Gentlemen don't work.

Basil Gentlemen do this kind of work. We've got to go and give something to the serfs.

Boris (*sitting up with interest*) Oh, really? What are we going to give them this time? Six of the best with a knotted rope, eh?

Basil No, no, we're going to give them Christmas presents

Boris (*lying back down again*) Christmas presents? Forget it.

Basil If we don't do it, Boris, Daddy will be extremely angry. And, if Daddy's extremely angry, then we'll be the ones who get six of the best with a knotted rope.

In reaction to this threat, Boris leaps down from the stove in one clean movement and lands beside his brother

Boris Right, off we go then. By the way, Basil old chap, what are the Christmas presents we're going to give all the serfs?
Basil (*picking up from the floor a large leather bag with a drawstring mouth and moving forward*) We're going to give them—sweeties!

As the two brothers move forward, a snow-covered forest cloth comes across behind them, hiding the sitting-room set

SCENE 2

In front of the snow-covered forest cloth

The action is continuous from the previous scene, as Basil and Boris step forward

Boris Sweeties? Did you say "sweeties"?
Basil Yes. (*He opens the bag*) Have a look.
Boris (*looking inside the bag*) I like sweeties.
Basil So do I. (*He looks inside the bag too*) Very much.

They exchange looks

It would be awfully naughty.
Boris Oh yes. No, we mustn't even think of it.
Basil I mean, we've got so much, and the poor serfs have got so little.
Boris Exactly.
Basil On the other hand, they'd never know.

As Basil works out his selfish logic, Boris becomes aware of the audience, and moves slowly and curiously downstage to look at them

And what they don't know about's not going to worry them… I mean, it might actually be bad for the serfs to think they'll always be getting sweeties… (*He reaches into the bag and pulls out a sweetie. He looks at it with relish as he talks*) I mean, in fact, we'd really be doing them a favour if we ate all the sweeties. (*He lifts the sweetie towards his mouth, as if about to eat it*) And the thing is, the serfs can't see what we're doing, so——
Boris (*suddenly, pointing at the audience in a wide gesture*) Ooh, look at all those serfs out there!
Basil (*doing an elaborate take and shoving the sweetie back into the bag*)

What! (*He turns a charmingly patronising smile on the audience*) Well, hell-ooo. We've been looking for you all over the place. We're so keen to give you all these sweeties. (*He smiles even more ingratiatingly*) I say— what a splendid looking lot of serfs you are. Really made an effort with dressing up, haven't you? I mean, in this light, some of you hardly look like peasants at all. (*Very patronising*) Well done. (*He rubs his hands together*) All right, come on then, Boris, let's start giving out these sweeties, shall we? Boris...?

But he gets no response. Boris has once again fallen asleep, standing up and snoring slightly

Boris! Boris!!

Still no reaction

(*Turning back to the audience*) Sorry, I'm afraid my brother has got rather a habit of going to sleep at important moments. I shout at him, but it has no effect. (*A thought comes to him*) I say, I wonder if all you serfs would like to help me? Yes, that would be great. Look, do you think, if you ever see my brother dropping off to sleep, you could all call out "Wake up, Boris!" Would you do that for me? Oh, terrific, well done. Shall we give it a try? See if we can wake him up now, eh? Yes? All right, on a count of three... One—two—three!

The audience shouts "Wake up, Boris!" but there is no reaction from Boris

Oh, look, come on! That wouldn't wake up a dormouse. Let's try again-and really loud this time! On a count of three... One—two—three!

The audience shouts again. This time Boris wakes up with a jolt, and looks around him in surprise

Boris Ooh! What's going on?
Basil I was just about to give out all these sweeties to the lovely serfs.
Boris But I thought you said you were going to eat them all yoursel——
Basil (*clapping his hand over Boris's mouth*) Shut up, Boris. Go back to sleep. (*He turns his ingratiating smile on the audience*)

During the ensuing speech, the Wolf enters and stands looming behind the two brothers

And now it's time for us to give out all these lovely sweeties. I do hope you realize how lucky you are.

While Basil talks on, Boris turns and sees the Wolf. He registers shock, looks back out front and shakes his head, as if dismissing the image from his mind

Other people's serfs live lives of cruelty and hardship. Whereas here on the Boronski estate you live in the lap of luxury, you're safe and protected.

Boris turns round again and sees the Wolf. There's no mistaking it this time

There's nothing here that can do you any harm at all.

Boris (*tapping his brother on the shoulder*) Except the w-w-w-w-w-w-w——

Basil The w-w-w-w-w-w-w-what?

Boris The w-w-w-w-w-w-w-Wolf.

Basil The Wolf? Don't be ridiculous. We Boronskis' ve hunted all the wolves off our estate. (*He appeals to the audience*) There aren't any wolves here, are there, serfs?

Audience reaction—"behind you, behind you", etc.

What, behind me? Don't be ridiculous. There's nothing behind me. (*He turns round elaborately, comes face to face with the Wolf, but turns back unaffected by the sight*) See, there's nothing there. Well, only a... (*Sudden panic take*) WOLF!!

Boris and Basil both try to rush off the stage in opposite directions. They cannon into each other c and fall to the ground. The Wolf steps forward and picks them up by the scruffs of their necks. He holds them, dangling, one either side of him, and looks at them sternly

Wolf So ... there aren't any wolves here, are there?

Boris Aagh! It can talk!

Basil (*gibbering to the Wolf*) Well, I mean obviously I was generalising. What I meant is there aren't many wolves here. But clearly there is one ... at least ... you... (*With a big, simpering smile*) and may I say how very pleased we are to see you.

Boris (*also with a big, simpering smile*) Oh yes, absolutely frightfully chuffed.

Basil Mm. Well um, I wonder ... Mr Wolf ... what can we do for you?

Wolf You can provide my dinner for me.

Basil Yes, fine. I don't think that should be too much of a problem. The servants can rustle up some beetroot soup and some nice game pie with——

Wolf No. I meant you can provide my dinner for me in a more immediate way.

Basil In a more immediate way?
Boris I wonder what he means by that?
Wolf I mean ... you ... will ... be ... my dinner.
Basil (*little shriek*) Aah!
Boris (*little shriek*) Ooh!
Wolf Now ... the only question is ... which one of you will I eat first...?
Basil ⎫ (*together*) ⎧ Oh, I'm in no rush. You can do me any time.
Boris ⎭   ⎩ Why not start with Basil? He's the oldest.
Wolf (*releasing his hold on Basil and turning beadily to Boris*) I think I'll eat you first.

Basil tries to crawl away, but the Wolf puts a foot on his leg to immobilise him

Boris That's awfully generous of you, and obviously I'm frightfully honoured, but I don't mind if——
Basil (*looking at the bag of sweeties, which he's still holding, and getting an idea*) I say I've had a thought of something else you can eat, Mr Wolf.
Wolf Hmm?
Basil (*holding the bag of sweeties out*) Do you like sweeties?

The Wolf lets out a roar and grabs the bag of sweeties. He tears open the top and looks down at his booty. Boris and Basil take advantage of the moment to break free

Quick, Boris—home!
Boris You bet!

Basil and Boris rush off

The Wolf notices this, and growls. But he is not too disappointed. He has, after all, got the bag of sweeties

Wolf Oh, never mind. I'll have these sweeties as a starter, and then catch those two nice juicy boys to be my main course. (*He reaches into the sweetie bag to take some out, then becomes aware of the audience*) Or, I wonder... Maybe I should give some of these sweeties to all you poor serfs out there...? Do you think I should...? (*He reaches into the bag, takes out a handful of sweeties and makes as if to throw them*) It would be a really kind thing to do, wouldn't it? (*He stops in mid-throw and grins wickedly*) Except, of course, that I'm a wolf, and it goes against my nature to be kind. No, you lot won't ever get any sweeties from me! Certainly not! No. Ha, ha, ha, I'm going to eat them all myself!

With an evil laugh, the Wolf goes off, cramming sweeties into his mouth—hopefully to a chorus of boos and hisses from the audience

SCENE 3

The Boronskis' sitting-room

The cloth draws back to reveal Katerina and Natasha sitting lazily with cups of tea. Natasha is reading a novel. The stove glows and the samovar steams comfortingly behind them

Katerina (*lethargically, holding out her cup*) I'd quite like another cup of tea.
Natasha (*equally lethargically, holding out her cup without looking up from her book*) So would I.

There is a silence. They eye the samovar, which is almost within touching distance of both of them

Katerina Why is there never a servant around when you need one? (*She calls off*) Olga! Masha! Irena!
Natasha Irena! Masha! Olga!
Katerina Where are they all?

Boris and Basil burst in, gibbering with fear

Basil Mummy! Natasha! It's terrible!
Katerina (*without stirring from her lethargy*) I agree. What on earth do the servants expect—that we're going to get up and pour out our own tea?
Basil No, no! What we've seen is terrible!
Boris We've seen a w-w-w-w-w-w-w——
Katerina A *w*aiting-woman, I hope.
Boris No, a w-w-w-w-w-w-w——
Basil A wolf.
Natasha (*still reading*) Don't be ridiculous. Father's huntsmen chased all the wolves off our estates years ago.
Basil Well, there's definitely one here now—a big, cruel, wicked wolf.
Boris (*almost crying*) And he's stolen all our sweeties!
Katerina All your sweeties?
Boris All the serfs' sweeties.
Basil And he said he was going to eat us.
Katerina Said? Are you telling me this wolf you met could talk? Have you two boys been at the vodka again?
Basil No, Mummy, honestly.
Katerina You must've been if you imagine that dumb animals can talk. That's why they're called "dumb". Nobody's ever seen an animal that can talk.

*There is a puff of smoke, keyboard underscore, and the Fox appears on
stage. She is beautiful, sexy, mystical and evil, with a magnificently bushy
tail*

*Boris and Basil start gibbering again and cower away from her. Katerina
and Natasha are less impressed*

Fox   Countess Boronski, do not be so sure
                                 You'll soon see many things you've never seen
                                 before.
Katerina (*rising languidly from her seat and moving towards the Fox*)
Honestly, you two boys are just so ignorant. This isn't a wolf, it's a fox.
Look, it's got a great long, bushy tail. Didn't those tutors of yours teach you
any natural history? (*She turns back to Boris and Basil*) This is just a
perfectly ordinary, common-or-garden fox.
Basil (*gulping nervously*) Except that it can talk.
Katerina (*matter-of-factly*) Yes, of course, except that it can talk. (*She does
a sudden delayed take and looks back at the Fox in horror*) Oh dear.

*Natasha, suddenly afraid, puts down her book, and all the Boronskis back
fearfully away from the Fox*

Fox   Why, yes, Boronskis, you do well to cower.
                                 I am the Fox, and you are in my power.
                                 No feeble human forces can prevail
                                 Against the witchcraft in my magic tail.
                                 The Wolf exists—he's my obedient slave.
                                 Whose fierce jaws will be your lasting grave.
                                 You are bewitched! There's nothing you can do.
                                 The Fox and Wolf will be the end of you.
Katerina Nonsense! My husband will hunt you off his land.
Fox   He will not, Countess. You must understand—
                                 Your husband's trapped—I've caught him in my
                                    spell.
                                 He won't come back. You've said your last farewell.
                                 I'm now in charge. You're in my stranglehold,
                                 And I condemn you to eternal cold!

*The Lighting changes to a harsher, colder glare. The sound of a keening wind
is heard. The Boronskis wrap their arms around themselves against the
sudden chill*

(*With a gesture to the samovar*) Your tea will freeze!

A magical chord is heard. The steam from the samovar immediately ceases, and the samovar falls over

(*With a gesture to the stove*) Your stove will cease to glow!

Another chord. The warm glow from the stove instantly vanishes

Your shutters won't keep out the cruel snow!

A third chord. The shutters and windows blow open. A gust of snow blows in

You'll not defeat my magic, it's so clever.
Spring will not come, and winter last for ever!

Strange, unearthly music underscores the ensuing action

Natasha But surely——
Fox   Silence! No more words! Be dumb!
You'll all be frozen now till kingdom come!

Boris, you first. Approach, and in a trice
You'll be transformed into a block of ice.

Boris, unable to resist the magic, moves forward, zombie-like, and freezes in a rigid pose. His eyes close

Katerina ⎫
Natasha ⎬ (*together*) Oh, look, please, have mercy… (*Etc.*)
Basil   ⎭
Fox   You other three, your piteous pleas I spurn!
Obey my spell! To icy statues turn!

Katerina, Natasha and Basil are unable to resist the magic. At a gesture from the Fox, they freeze in whatever positions they happen to be

You're trapped! It's done! Life's over for you all!
Remember this—pride comes before a fall!

The Fox goes into her version of the Boronskis' opening song

No. 2: Winter's Ending, Spring is Coming (Fox's Version)
You're the Boronskis, eternally cursed,
No longer living in clover

Your bubble of wealth and possessions has burst;
Your days of good fortune are over.
Those who meet the Fox's magic
Find their future very tragic,
With all the pain my evil powers can bring.
Now for ever they will languish
With a cold, unending anguish
And in vain will keep on longing for the spring.

Winter stays, and spring is cancelled.
Now the ice will never thaw,
No plants grow
Up through the snow,
And a cruel frost brings more
Winter whiteness.
Summer's brightness
Never will come through your door.

With a defiant gesture, and in another puff of smoke, the Fox vanishes

SCENE 4

In front of the snow-covered forest cloth

The Wolf enters, still clutching the bag of sweeties

Wolf I've still only eaten one or two of these sweeties. (*He reaches into the bag and pulls out a handful*) Shall I eat all the rest now? Oh, I think I will. Don't you? Because I'm a wicked wolf—and that's the sort of thing wicked wolves do.

The Fox enters behind him

The Wolf is very respectful when he sees her

Fox   No, it is not. What wicked wolves should eat is
                             Live human beings, not human beings' sweeties.
Wolf But surely, if I just have one or two——
Fox   No, none at all, not when you've work to do.
Wolf What work?
Fox   Whatever task I choose to give.
                             You're in my power, and if you want to live,
                             You will obey my every decree.

> Throughout all Russia now just you and me
> Will rule the folk by fear and by deceit.
> Those who resist or argue … you will eat.

Wolf (*licking his lips*) That does sound fun. When do I start?
Fox   Right now. Soon, following my magic art,
> To the Boronskis' house you must make tracks,
> Where I've prepared you four deep-frozen snacks.

The Wolf licks his lips again

> But first, your wicked appetite to whet,
> There's an old lady here who must be ate.
> Natasha's grandmother can start your lunch
> And on her ancient bones your teeth can crunch.
> She lives nearby—go, find her cottage fast!
> She'll be the first you eat…

The Wolf howls in delighted anticipation

> …but not the last!

The Fox disappears in a puff of smoke; scene change music (2a)

The Wolf, all psyched up and hungry, roars and rushes offstage

Scene 5

Babushka's sitting-room

This set, like the Boronskis', is dominated by a large stove, but everything is on a much less lavish scale. Though the room is quite cosily appointed, the cottage is only one step up from a hovel. The windows are shuttered

When the cloth draws back, the room is empty, but then Babushka enters in her bed. She has a large piece of knitting with her

Babushka (*addressing the audience directly*) Oh, hallo, serfs! What a lovely lot of serfs you are—a positive surfeit of serfs. I'm Babushka, by the way. Yes, Babushka. Don't you understand? Honestly, you lot are ignorant. It's Russian. What do you think it means? (*Mock-affront*) No, it does not mean "baboon". It means "grandmother"—right, got that?

Yes, I'm Boris's and Basil's and Natasha's grandmother. (*She does a little pirouette in her mobile bed*) Like the bed, do you? I had it designed specially. Well, you see, I'm one of those people who always likes to be up to something, but who doesn't like getting up.

Very practical in this kind of climate, too, staying in bed all the time. I tell you, round here it's so cold outside that ... well, let's just say that most gentlemen wait till they get home to spend a rouble. No, it can get very nippy round the Urals. (*She reacts to someone in the audience*) Oy, oy, no, thank you, this is not that kind of pantomime.

(*She bounces out of bed to reveal stripy bloomers*) Like the bloomers, do you? Knitted them myself. I'm a great knitter, you know.

(*She puts on a dress as she continues talking to the audience*) You've met my daughter Katerina, haven't you? Countess "Oh-I-can't-mix-with-all-those-vulgar-people" Boronski. Load of nonsense, all that is. She's no more aristocratic than I am. Just a nice normal night-watchman's niece from Nishni-Novgorod—and don't try saying that after you've been at the vodka. No, she just married lucky, my Katya. "Katya" I call her. None of this Oh-my-Gawd "Countess Boronski, wife of Count Sergei Boronski" stuff for me. Just "Katya". (*With relish*) Makes her furious.

Trouble is, she doesn't do what most kids who're social climbers do. Most of them just cut themselves off from their family. But not Katya. Tell you, it'd be quite a relief if she did. But no, Katya keeps in touch with me all the time. She's always worrying about me. Honestly, why doesn't the girl give me a break and let me get on with my own life? Hah one—two—three—and into my song...

No. 3: Why Won't the Young Leave the Old Folks Alone?

(*Spoken*) Why won't the young leave the old folks alone?
Why won't they let me have a life of my own?
(*Singing*) To put the thing succinctly,
They say 'cos I'm a wrinklie
That I'm therefore quite incapable of thought.
But if they knew the truth,
They'd not set such store by youth,
'Cos the skills that I've developed can't be bought...

I can always spot a liar;
I'm shrewder and I'm flyer;
My wit is so much drier—

And in matters of desire
I'm the last one to retire.
Like wine I've just got better the older I've grown
But, because I'm sixty-plus,
All my children fret and fuss—
They won't listen, won't discuss.
Still, I fear 'twas ever thus...
Oh, why won't the young leave the old folks alone?

She does a little dance

Why won't the young leave the old folks alone?
Why do they always disapprove and moan?
Whenever I get frisky,
They say it's awfully risky
And I really should behave and act my age,
But what they cannot see
Is that I feel twenty-three
And I'm not yet prepared to leave the stage!
Oh when my daughter mothers me, well, sometimes
    I could strike her...
(*She winks*) 'Cos there's many a good tune played
    on an old balalaika.
Come, sing it once again and move it up a semitone!
OH, WHY WON'T THE YOUNG LEAVE THE
    OLD FOLKS ALONE!!

*She sings with the audience, then at the end of the song bounces back into her
bed*

*Ivan enters through the front door, carrying a pile of logs. He is a
handsome woodcutter, humbly dressed in peasant clothes. He carries his
axe in a leather holder on his belt*

Good morning, Ivan.
Ivan I've brought some wood for your stove.
Babushka Oh, bless you. I do appreciate all you've done for me through the
    winter, but don't worry, soon you can stop, Ivan. Soon it will be spring.
Ivan Yes. (*He starts to stack up the logs, then asks casually*) Has Natasha
    been to see you recently?
Babushka No. (*She looks him in the eye*) You aren't still thinking about her,
    are you?
Ivan Some things just don't go away, I'm afraid.

Babushka For heaven's sake, Ivan! Forget about her. You're totally wrong for each other.

Ivan Why—because she's an aristocrat and I'm just a humble woodcutter?

Babushka No, because you're a fine, intelligent young man, and she's a spoilt little brat.

Ivan But I still love her. (*Idealistically*) Maybe, if I keep on trying to educate myself, one day she'll look at me differently...?

Babushka (*cynically, as she gets out of bed again*) Oh yes, and maybe one day pigs'll fly.

Ivan Well, I was always told that one must never give up hope.

Babushka Who told you that then?

Ivan My... I always want to say "my father", but I suppose it should be "the old man who brought me up". A forester. He died two years ago. He was more than a father to me.

Babushka How did he come to bring you up?

Ivan He found me in the forest when I was a baby.

Babushka What, just lying there—like a fir cone or something?

Ivan Yes. Before he died, the old man gave me many things. Many magic things.

Babushka Magic things? What, like conjuring tricks?

Ivan No, magic things like a book of spells—and magic powder—and a magic stick. And also—this axe. (*He draws it out to show her*)

Babushka And what magic does that do—saw ladies in half?

Ivan No. When someone the owner loves is in danger, the axe-head glows red.

Babushka (*taking the axe from him and poo-pooing the idea*) "When someone the owner loves is in danger, the axe-head glows red"?

As she speaks the axe-head begins to glow red

Honestly, I've never heard such a load of absolute... (*Her words peter out as she notices the glowing axe-head*)

Ivan turns to see it too

Ivan Oh no, it must be Natasha! I will protect you, my dearest!

Ivan seizes the axe and rushes off stage

Babushka What rubbish. The things young people believe nowadays. I blame these new novels that keep being published. Kids just mooch around all day gazing at the printed page—it can't do them any good, can it? If you want my opinion, literature rots the brain.

*The Wolf sneaks on through the front door, upstage of Babushka. He is
still carrying his bag of sweeties*

Babushka does not see him

It's not natural, reading—it can't be. If God had intended us to read, he
wouldn't have given us ears, would he? (*She turns to the audience*) What,
are you trying to tell me something? Beware of what? A wolf? Don't be
ridiculous. All right, if there's a wolf, where is it? (*Very slowly she turns
round in a complete circle*)

The Wolf scuttles out of the front door before she sees him

I can't see anything. Where is this wolf? (*She looks out of the front door*)
See—there's nothing there.

*As soon as she faces downstage again, the Wolf comes back in and towers
over her*

Oh, you do make a fuss, you lot. There isn't any wolf in——

The audience will hopefully shout "Behind you! Behind you!"

Where? (*She turns back to the doorway*)

Once again, the Wolf scuttles out of sight

Babushka has another look out of the door, then turns back downstage

*As soon as she does so, the Wolf scuttles across the stage to hide behind
her bed*

As she speaks, he emerges from behind the bed to stand directly behind her

Goodness, you lot have got fertile imaginations. Scare yourself silly, you
will.

*The Wolf taps her on the shoulder. She brushes it off as if something had
dropped on her*

Oh, these spiders keep dropping down from the rafters, you know.

The Wolf taps her on the other shoulder. She brushes that off too

Dear me, there's another one.

The audience: "Behind you! Behind you!"

Behind me? Don't be ridiculous. (*She turns round to look straight at the Wolf, then turns back, unworried*) See—there's nothing there, is there? Nothing, except, of course, for a… (*Her words trickle away, as she gulps*) …big, huge, ferocious, wicked wolf.

The Wolf roars right behind her. Babushka shoots up in the air, scuttles across the stage, then turns back to face the Wolf, with a sickly grin on her face

Is there anything you want to do with me, Mr Wolf?
Wolf Yes, I want to eat you.
Babushka (*little shriek*) Oh, well, fancy that.
Wolf Yes, I do. Very much. (*He advances on Babushka*)

She backs away and gets the bed between them. They circle round this during the ensuing dialogue, moving slowly towards the front door

Babushka You wouldn't really want to eat me, you know.
Wolf Oh, yes, I would!
Babushka Oh, no, you wouldn't!
Wolf Oh yes, I would!
Babushka Oh no, you wouldn't!
Wolf Oh yes, I would!!
Babushka Oh no, you wouldn't!!
Wolf Oh yes, I would!!
Babushka I say, I've suddenly had a thought…
Wolf What?
Babushka If you did eat me…
Wolf Yes?
Babushka …then you'd be eating something that disagreed with you. (*She laughs at her little joke*)

The Wolf is momentarily non-plussed by this. Babushka seizes the opportunity to shove him out of the front door, slam it, and fix the bar across it. She slaps her hands together with satisfaction

I don't know. Even the wolves are looking younger these days. (*She leaps back into her mobile bed and propels herself across the stage, waving*) Bye bye, everyone. Bye bye!

Babushka exits

SCENE 6

In front of the snow-covered forest cloth

The Fox enters in a puff of smoke, magnificent and triumphant

Music underscores the Fox's words

No. 4: Fox's Speech

Fox (*singing*)   My spells begin to do their wicked work.
                          Good can't survive when evil goes berserk.
                          The grandmother's been eaten in her bed,
                          And soon the young Boronskis will be dead.

The Wolf enters, looking sorry for himself

(*Speaking*) Say, slave, and have you done the Fox's bidding?
Wolf Er, well, not quite.
Fox   Not quite? I hope you're kidding.
Wolf The old girl caught me out—she was too quick.
Fox (*furious*)   And you fell for the simplest human trick?
Wolf I'm sorry. I just——
Fox (*now icily calm*)   Do not be concerned.
                          Your feebleness to fury will be turned.
                          (*She produces a small pie to offer him*)
                          When you taste this, your powers will gain renewal,
                          You'll be more fierce, more merciless, more cruel
                          Than all the monsters horror-tales can fashion.
                          You will forget the meaning of compassion.
Wolf What's in the pie?
Fox   Don't ask! Just take and eat!
                          (*She hands the pie across*)
                          And then my murderous plan will be complete.

The Wolf takes the pie. He takes a tentative nibble, then roars with delight at the taste and, ferocious and slavering, wolfs (well, he would, wouldn't he?) down the rest

Wolf What is it? What is it? The taste is quite sublime. I want some more!
Fox   You'll get some more in time.

It's like a drug. At first you find it pleasant...
Take it or leave it ... not as nice as pheasant...
But then you're hooked. A mouthful of the stuff
No longer works—it isn't quite enough...
You need that crunchy taste within your jaw...
You need some more... Then more! And more! And
more!
Your hunger grows till, desperate with haste,
You will do anything to get that taste.
To greed alone your will becomes obedient,
And all you crave for is that one ingredient.

Wolf (*desperate*) What is it? What is in the pie? I have to know.

Fox   I'll tell you. And you'll want it so
You'll go straight off to get some nice and fresh.
What you are hooked on, Wolf, is—human flesh!

The Wolf roars ravenously

Wolf Look out, Boronskis—for your days are done!

The Wolf rushes off, roaring, desperate for more human flesh

No. 4a: Fox's Speech (continued)

Fox (*singing*)   The Fox's rule of terror has begun.
Prayers will not work—no hope for "Lord, deliver
us",
Now that the Wolf is totally carnivorous!

The Fox leaves the stage in triumph

Scene 7

The Boronskis' sitting-room

The cloth draws back to reveal the four family members frozen in exactly the positions they were at the end of Scene 3. More snow has blown in through the open window and is dusted over the stove and furniture. A chill wind keens. An air of desolation hangs over everything

A moment is allowed for the audience to take in the scene; then Ivan bursts in downstage, wielding his still-glowing axe

Ivan Oh, no! They have been enchanted by some evil sorceress. Still, I must fight enchantment with enchantment. I'm sure there's something in the old forester's book of spells. (*He takes out his book of spells*) Just a matter of finding the right one... (*He flicks through the book until he finds what he's looking for. Then he steps forward towards the frozen Boronskis, and is inevitably drawn to Natasha*) Oh, you are so beautiful. So beautiful when you are like this—when you are silent and cannot show how proud you are. But how should I wake you? Well, of course, in the story of *Sleeping Beauty*... (*He is about to kiss her, but then stops himself*) No, Natasha, my love, I will not kiss you until you want to kiss me too. (*Dreamily*) And I firmly believe that somehow that day will come. (*He becomes brisk and businesslike*) But now let's try my axe's powers. (*He consults the book of spells, then swings the axe to either side of Natasha as he sings the charm*)

No. 4b: Ivan's Magic Spell
"Reverse the spells of witches' wands,
And, magic axe, undo her bonds!"

As he speaks the final words, Natasha unfreezes and looks around her in bewilderment. For a moment, Ivan is about to say something to her, but then he moves on to complete his task. Swinging his axe to either side of the other three he sings the charm

"Reverse the spells of witches' wands,
And, magic axe, undo their bonds!"

As he speaks the final words, Katerina and Basil come back to life and, like Natasha, look around them in bewilderment. Boris, however, remains frozen in exactly the same position

Katerina (*hugging herself against the cold*) Well, about time too, Ivan.
Natasha Yes, what took you so long? (*She picks up her novel and slumps languidly into a chair*) I was just getting to an interesting bit in my novel. (*She starts reading*)
Ivan (*becoming aware of Boris*) But one of you is still enchanted.
Basil Don't you believe it. If I know Boris, he just fell asleep while he was under the spell. (*To the audience*) All right, we all know what to do, don't we? One—two—three!

The audience shout "Wake up, Boris!" Sure enough, Boris comes back to life, and looks around him in puzzlement

Boris (*thoughtfully, as he pieces it together*) Do you know, I've just had the most peculiar dream... I dreamt that someone was coming to eat me...

Basil Who?

Boris (*suddenly terrified as he remembers*) It was the w-w-w-w-w-w-w——

Katerina When are those servants going to appear? This room's an absolute shambles. All that snow needs sweeping out.

Basil Yes, and I'm jolly hungry.

Natasha (*looking up from her book and calling offstage*) Olga! Masha! Irena! Oh, for heaven's sake—where are those wretched girls?

Ivan (*moving towards Natasha*) Milady, don't you think you should be checking——

Basil (*to Ivan*) You go and tell the servants to bring us something to eat, Ivan—and sharpish. Nothing elaborate, mind, just a snack. (*He leads into a song*)

	No. 5: Just a Little Snack
	Bring us a little chicken...
Boris	And some turkey and some duck...
Katerina	And some quail and grouse and partridge...
Natasha	And some pheasant
	Just for luck!
Basil (*to Boris*)	You'd like some rabbit pie
	If my guess is not mistaken...
Boris	And lovely, lovely, lovely, lovely
	Egg and sausage and bacon.
Katerina	And bring some strawberry vodka
	As a nice aperitif...
Basil	And a little bit of gammon...
Boris	And some brisket...
Natasha	And some beef!
Boris	I'd like a whole wild boar...
Basil	You really are a glutton.
Boris	And lamb that is scrumptious and gorgeous and succulent...
Katerina	Rubbish, you'll settle for mutton.
Natasha	Our stomachs are so empty.
	I'll tell you what we lack—
All Boronskis	Just a little snack, Ivan,
	Just a little snack.
Katerina	So hurry off and get it
	And bring it quickly back!
All Boronskis	Just a little snack, Ivan,
	Just a little snack.

Ivan goes into his more serious song. At first the Boronskis listen to him, but they soon lose interest

Ivan   Don't you think you ought to
                            Barricade the doors?
                            Shouldn't you have thought to
                            Safeguard what is yours?
                            There's a fox outside
                            Who's mysterious.
                            And a wolf too—
                            This is serious.
                            When there's so much unpleasantness...
                            Should you think of food at a time like...?

Katerina comes straight back into her song without reacting to Ivan's

Katerina   Let's have some apple pudding...
Natasha   And some bread and strawberry jam...
Basil   And a side of pickled salmon...
Boris   And some haddock...
Natasha   And some ham!
Katerina   I'd like a cup of tea
                            That is steamy, hot and hissing.
                            (*She gets very operatic*) And samovar, samovar,
                                samovar, samovar...
                            (*Sudden bathos as she notices the absence of the
                                cups*) Tea cups are missing.

During the last chorus, Ivan sings his song at the same time, and the two melodies mingle

Natasha Our stomachs are so   **Ivan** There's a fox outside
        empty.   Who's mysterious
    I'll tell you what we   And a wolf too—
        lack—   This is serious.
All Boronskis Just a little snack,   When there's so much
        Ivan,   unpleasantness...
    Just a little snack.   Should you think of food
Katerina So hurry off and get it   at a time like...?
    And bring it quickly   (*Spoken*) At a time like
        back!   this
All Just a little snack, Ivan   At a time like this
    Just a little snack   At a time like this
    Just a little snack, just   Aah!

a little snack
Just a little (*spoken*)
snack snack snack

At the end of the song, Ivan, exasperated by their lack of reaction to his warnings, exits

Katerina Well, how very tedious all that being frozen business was. And Ivan certainly took his time coming to rescue us.
Boris Yes... On the other hand, he did save our lives. Don't you think we ought to say thank you to him?
Katerina Say thank you to a serf? Boris, honestly, all that money your father and I spent on your education and you come up with something like that.
Natasha Yes, sometimes, Boris, you're just so uncouth.

Boris looks suitably chastened

Ivan enters, looking shocked

Ivan Countess, all the servants have run away.
Katerina Run away?
Ivan Yes. And all the food has vanished from the store-rooms.
Basil (*very put out*) But what about our little snack?
Ivan All your money's gone, Countess. Your jewels and silver have been stolen too!
Katerina What're we supposed to live on then? If we haven't got any money.
Ivan Many people in this country live on what they can find in the fields and forests.
Katerina I dare say they do, but not people of our class. And if you think I'm going to start living on stale bread and root vegetables, you've got another think coming. (*She shivers and wraps her arms around herself*) It's cold, too. Ivan, go and get some more wood for the stove.
Ivan But, Countess, don't you think you should——
Katerina Go and get some more wood for the stove!
Ivan Yes, Countess.

Grimly, Ivan picks up his axe and goes off

Katerina (*putting her hand to her temple*) Oh dear, I'm afraid all this is bringing on one of my migraines. I'll have to go upstairs and lie down.
Basil But what should we do?
Katerina I don't know. Find us some food for a start, I would think.
Basil Yes, yes, of course. (*He pauses*) How?
Katerina Oh, for heaven's sake, Basil! Haven't you got any initiative?

Basil Erm… No, I don't think I probably have. Daddy was always the one with initiative, wasn't he?

Katerina Goodness, you're hopeless.

Boris (*hoping to ingratiate himself*) Yes, he is, isn't he?

Katerina And you're no better!

Boris Oh.

Katerina (*on her way out*) Oh, I wish Sergei was here…

Katerina exits

Natasha (*looking up from her novel*) Well, come on. Between the two of you, you should be able to work out some ideas for making money, shouldn't you?

Basil Yes. Yes, you're right, we should. (*He pauses, then, less certain*) Shouldn't we? You haven't got any ideas, have you, Boris?

Boris No.

Basil Don't know why I bothered asking.

Boris (*squaring up to his brother*) Now don't you start being rude to me, Basil. I'll jolly well——

Natasha Look, will you two stop squabbling and do something! There's an emergency here. We haven't got any food.

Basil That's true. That's very true. We must do something about it. (*Bustling and businesslike*) Don't worry, I'm in charge here. I'll find us some food. (*He pauses*) Natasha, have you any ideas where we might find some food?

Natasha Well, you could go fishing, couldn't you?

Basil Yes, we could. I've just had an idea, Boris.

Boris What?

Basil We'll go fishing.

Boris But that wasn't your——

Basil (*leading his brother off*) Shut up! Let's go and find our fishing tackle! Rods, reels, hooks, floats…

Boris So that we can get something to eat…

Basil …worms…

Boris (*on his way out*) I'm not going to eat worms!

Boris and Basil exit

Natasha shakes her head at her brothers' incompetence, sighs languidly, and returns to her book

Ivan enters, loaded down with wood. His axe is on his belt

Natasha does not look up. Ivan puts the wood down by the fire, and looks at Natasha. After a moment of indecision, he speaks

Ivan Natasha...
Natasha (*preoccupied*) Hmm?
Ivan Now that you're poor...
Natasha (*looking up*) What? I'm not poor.
Ivan I'm afraid you are. You'll need someone to protect you.
Natasha No, I won't. I'm a Boronski.
Ivan You will need someone, Natasha. You really will. And I'm volunteering.
Katerina Don't be ridiculous.
Ivan I don't mind that you're poor. It's not your wealth that I care about. I've always loved you for yourself. And I always will. (*He begins singing*)

No. 6: Unrequited Love Duet

Leaves will fall, and flowers fade,
And passions pass their prime
But, ever true, my love for you
Will stand the test of time.
Days must die, and evening's shade
Will darken with the dew,
But I'll love still, and wait until
You see my way too.

I don't want
A life with you
Until you want me
And love me too.
Oh, my darling,
Never fear—
If you need me,
I'll be here.

Natasha

You aren't my type, you aren't my class.
By God, you've got a nerve.
You're lucky Daddy's not around
To give what you deserve.
It's barefaced cheek for you to speak
To me and seek my hand.
Get off my turf—you're just a serf!
Why can't you understand...?

To be without you
Is my ideal
To marry you?
Here's what I feel—

I know my mind—
I do not love you.
Choose your own kind,
Not far above you.

Ivan   Flames will flicker, lights will dim,
                            And candles gutter out,
                            But, safe and sure, my dreams endure—
                            That you must never doubt.

Natasha   I know my mind—
                            I do not love you.
                            Choose your own kind,
                            Not far above you.

At the end of the song, Ivan looks wistfully at Natasha, but she turns her head proudly away from him

Ivan goes off sadly

Natasha picks up her novel, opens it and sits down to continue reading

Katerina enters, carrying a basket with a white cloth over it

Katerina Natasha, have Basil and Boris thought of any way of getting food?
Natasha They're going fishing.
Katerina Oh, good heavens, if we have to wait till those two catch something, we'll certainly starve. I've had an idea.
Natasha What?
Katerina Your Babushka will have some food. She's always well stocked. (*She hands the basket across*) You take this and get her to load it up with goodies for us.
Natasha But she'll make awful fun of me if she thinks we're reduced to begging.
Katerina I don't care what she thinks! Go and get some food! We're starving!

Natasha moves grudgingly towards the door

And put your red riding hood on!
Natasha Oh, do I have to?
Katerina You certainly do, my girl. It's way below freezing out there.
Natasha (*putting on her red riding hood with bad grace*) I don't know. Red's

so unfashionable this year. And anything knitted's totally out. (*On her way out*) Oh, dear, I look like an accident in a dressmaker's shop. Life is hell.

Natasha exits

Katerina Yes, isn't it just? And goodness knows what this unending winter's going to do to the cherry orchard... My migraine's not getting any better, either. (*Tragically, as she comes downstage*) Dear, oh, dear—is there to be no end to my suffering?

As Katerina moves forward, a cloth of Katerina's bedroom comes across the stage

SCENE 8

Katerina's bedroom

The action is continuous. Katerina looks extremely sorry for herself

Katerina Oh, and the mere idea of poverty... (*She shudders*) For the Countess Boronski, wife of Count Sergei Boronski ... it just doesn't bear thinking of...

No. 7: Keeping the Wolf from the Door
For someone of my background,
Who never saw it coming,
To have to pass the hat round.
It's demeaning—well, it's slumming...
And just to think of money
Is a fate beyond reclaiming.
It's embarrassing and bourgeois—
Oh, my dears, it's too, too shaming.

We used to have ten servants—
Now that's reduced to four.
No wonder I'm obsessed with
Keeping the wolf from the door.

Just the thought of me not dressed in
The latest Paris fashion
Brings a pain to my intestine,
Makes my face turn ashen.

To have to darn a stocking
Would not amuse me vastly.
It's appalling, it's shocking,
No, in fact it's simply ghastly.

I used to dress in satins,
Brocades and furs galore,
But I'll end up wearing sacking,
Keeping the wolf from the door.

Katerina dances

I once had maids to dress me
And do every household chore,
But I could now end up... (*with distaste*) working
Keeping the wolf from the door.

Katerina goes off, sobbing with self-pity

SCENE 9

The frozen lake

On the sparkling icy beauty of the lake, the **Duck Dance** *(No. 8) takes place. A mother duck and her brood of tiny ducklings do a comic dance across the ice*

Suddenly, the Wolf appears and, with music matching the drama of the situation, chases the family of ducks

Feathers fly as the mother duck tries to protect her brood. The Wolf isolates the smallest duckling

In confusion, the mother and the rest of the brood manage to escape one side of the stage, while the Wolf chases the smallest duckling off the other side

Frantic high-pitched quacking is heard from offstage, followed by an ominous wolfish gulp, and a belch. A handful of feathers are thrown onstage from the wings

Then Basil and Boris come rushing on (music 8a), laden down with their fishing tackle. They skid about on the ice as they move. Boris carries a large rod, and amongst the items in Basil's bag is a large saw

Basil (*pointing after the ducks*) Duck! Duck!
Boris All right. (*He throws himself down on the ground with his hands over his head*)
Basil Not that kind of "duck", you fool!

Boris picks himself up

Boris, can I ask you something...?
Boris Mm?
Basil What is it like to be born the nearest thing to an idiot?
Boris Quite fun, actually. Must've been tough on you, though.
Basil On me? Why?
Boris Well, if I was born the nearest thing to an idiot ... and you were the nearest thing to me when I was born...
Basil Shut up, Boris! (*He looks up, as if seeing something invisible fly past in the sky*) Look! Duck!

Boris once again throws himself on the ground with his hands over his ears

No, you fool! Look, Boris, will you try and get this straight? When I say "duck", I don't mean "duck" like "throw yourself on the ground". I mean "duck" with beak and feathers. Still, never mind that. (*He takes a hammer and chisel out of his bag*) I'll make the hole in the ice. You put the bait on the hook.
Boris Bait? (*With distaste*) What, you mean one of the worms?
Basil Yes.
Boris But I hate worms. They're all horrid and wiggly.
Basil Just do it, Boris!
Boris All right, Basil. (*He starts going through the contents of the fishing bags. He overreacts with distaste to opening a tin of apparently wiggling worms*)

Basil, with his back to the audience to mask his actions, apparently chisels his way through the ice to make a hole. He talks while he hammers down on his chisel

Basil You know, they say that in this lake there lives a giant sturgeon.
Boris Oh, really?
Basil You do know what a sturgeon is, don't you, Boris?
Boris Of course I do, Basil.
Basil (*after a pause*) All right, what is it then?
Boris Honestly! Don't you know anything? A sturgeon is a chap who cuts you open, takes your insides out and sews you up again.

Basil No, it isn't, you idiot—that's a surgeon! A sturgeon is a fish. And do you know, the giant sturgeon that lives in this lake is supposed to have magic powers.

Boris I wish I had magic powers.

Basil Why?

Boris Because then I could magic this horrid, wiggly worm on to the hook without having to touch it.

Basil tuts in exasperation. Then he picks out what looks like a large disc of ice from the hole in the ice. He places this on the ground and turns with satisfaction to Boris

Basil Right, that's done. Is the worm on the hook yet, Boris?

Boris Not entirely.

Basil What do you mean—not entirely?

Boris Well, not at all, actually. You see, worms are so horrid and wiggly that——

Sighing with annoyance, Basil picks up the rod, holds it in the crook of his arm, and, without looking at Boris, holds out his hand for the worm

Basil Give it to me.

Boris reaches towards his brother. But the worm apparently starts to wriggle in Boris's hand. As he tries to control it, he steps on the disc of ice Basil has cut out of the lake

Boris skids offstage on it

(*Reaching his hand out to where Boris was*) All right, hand it over. Come on, Boris. (*He turns to look where his brother was*) Boris, where are you?

A crash and a scream from Boris is heard from offstage

Boris (*off; calling*) Don't worry—I'm coming back!

Boris comes skidding on from the wings on the ice-disc. But he has misjudged his pace and goes all the way across the stage

As Boris passes, Basil casually takes the worm from his hand

Basil Thank you. (*He attaches the worm to his hook*)

A crash and a scream from Boris is heard from the other side of the stage

(*Calling off*) Do try to stay upright, Boris. Look, get off the bit of ice. Then
you won't keep falling over.
Boris (*off; calling*) That's true. Here it comes!

*The ice-disc comes skidding across from the wings, catching Basil on the
back of the legs and sending him flying*

Boris enters and looks at his spread-eagled brother with amusement

(*Sniggering*) Do try to stay upright, Basil.

*Basil, silently fuming, picks himself up and deliberately lowers his baited
hook into the hole in the ice. The two brothers look down into the hole*

(*After a long pause*) Have you got a bite yet?
Basil (*short-tempered*) No, I haven't!
Boris (*after a long pause*) Not very interesting, fishing, is it? (*After another
long pause*) Don't you think you ought to check your worm's still on?
Basil Of course my worm's still on!
Boris (*after a pause*) You sure about that?
Basil Yes, of course I'm sure. (*He pulls the line out of the hole*) Do I have
to show you that... (*He looks at the end of the line*)

There is no worm on the hook

(*He concludes weakly*) ...there's no worm on the hook.

Boris grins smugly

Come on, I'll put another one on! (*He sits down and busies himself with
putting another worm on the hook*)

Boris goes upstage to look down the hole in the ice

Boris You know, I don't believe in this giant sturgeon. I think it's just another
of those fairy tales ... Like the witches' houses on chickens' legs, or the
story of the Tsar's son having been stolen from his cradle when he was a
baby...
Basil Well, the giant sturgeon is definitely supposed to exist. (*He stands up*)
There we are, I've got the hook baited again. (*He picks up the long rod,
tucks it underneath his arm, and cautiously moves round*) Duck, Boris.
Boris (*still with his back to his brother*) Nearly fell for it, Basil. But I know,
when you say "duck", you mean something with feathers and——

The rod catches him in the middle and tips him down the hole. Basil looks around for his vanished brother

Basil Oh, look, for heaven's sake, Boris. Where've you gone this time? (*He moves down to the edge of the stage to look for Boris*)

Boris pulls himself out of the hole and runs about the stage, shivering, teeth chattering

Boris Ooh, Basil, you did that on purpose!
Basil What?
Boris You deliberately knocked me down into the... Ow, I'm so cold. I'm going to get you, Basil. I'm going to push you down that hole!
Basil No! No!

Boris chases his brother round the stage

Katerina enters, and stands at the side of the stage with her arms folded, looking pityingly at the antics of her offspring

Basil sees her and comes to a skidding halt. Boris, who hasn't seen Katerina arrive, cannons into his brother's back. Both sprawl on the ground at their mother's feet

Katerina And may I ask what on earth you two think you're doing?
Basil Fishing, Mummy.
Boris (*picking himself up off the floor*) That's right, Mummy—fishing.
Katerina And have you caught anything?
Boris I think I've caught a cold.
Katerina Have you caught any fish?

Basil and Boris exchange looks

Basil ⎤
         ⎟ (*together*) We-ell...
Boris ⎦

No. 9: The One that Got Away

Basil	Whenever I go fishing...
Boris	It's the same for me as you...
Basil	My hook is neatly baited...
Boris	And my breath is bated too...
Basil	My float is sitting bobbing...
Boris	Then it gives a sudden twitch...
Basil	And I start to reel the line in...

Boris	Oh, isn't life a bitch!
Basil	Of course I'm never lucky
Boris	With despair I am consumed
	Tho' I try to keep my hopes up
Basil	Well I know that they'll be doomed
	'Cos by sea, or lake, or river…
Boris	Using fly, or worm, or bread…
Basil	The same thing always happens…
Boris	Yes, I fear, the fish, has fled…

Basil

I was fishing for a turbot,
And I felt a proper herbert
When my float bobbed down—imagine my dismay,
'Cos the fish would not be landed,
So it left me empty-handed—
But you should have seen the one that got away!

Oh, the one that got away—
It was a monster of perfection,
To be mounted in a case
In any fisherman's collection.
It resisted like a demon—
What a fighter—it was fat,
And, as for its dimensions…
(*With a traditional fisherman's arms wide gesture*)
It was twice as big as that!

Boris

If I'd only caught the monster… I'd be in the news
today;
The fish would have been stuffed and put on perma-
nent display.
So, though all I've got's a minnow, still I sadly have
to say…
Oh, you should have seen the one that got away!

Basil

I'm afraid I have to snigger,
'Cos the fish I catch are bigger
Than the ones that you go on about all day.

Boris

No, they're not. You do talk piffle.
You can't even catch a sniffle.
Well, I nearly caught the one that got away!

Basil
Boris } (*together*)   Oh, the one that got away——

Basil (*spoken*)   Ooh, it drove me really frantic.
                              It was huge, it was enormous!
Boris (*spoken*)   Well, my one was gigantic!
                              (*singing*) Oh, in fact it was so big it would
                              Make yours look like a sprat.
Basil   Mine, if it had been measured...
                              (*With a traditional fisherman's arms wide gesture*)
                              Would be four times more than that!

They both do the traditional fisherman's gesture as their claims get wilder

Boris (*spoken*)   Well, mine was five times more!
Basil (*spoken*)   Mine was six times more!
Boris (*spoken*)   Seven times!
Basil (*spoken*)   Eight times!
Boris (*spoken*)   Nine times!
Basil (*spoken*)   Ten!
Katerina (*at the top of her voice*) Will you two boys stop squabbling!
Basil   (*very subdued and soulfully*) Oh, just to catch a
                                  tiddler...
                              Would have really made my day...
Boris   Instead of looking mournful, I'd be shouting "Hip-
                                  hooray!"
Basil ⎤
Boris ⎦ (*together*)   But since we're so unlucky, can you blame us whe
                                  we say...

                              Oh, you should have seen the one that got away!
Basil (*spoken*)   It was titanic
Boris (*spoken*)   Oh tremendous
Basil (*spoken*)   Astonishing
Boris (*spoken*)   Stupendous
Katerina (*spoken*)   Oh, I wish I'd seen the one that got away

At the end of the song, as they form a tableau, the Giant Sturgeon rises up behind them from the hole in the ice, unseen by the three Boronskis. Then they turn round and see it, and all rush off in horror

Black-out

SCENE 10

In front of the snow-covered forest cloth

The Wolf enters, munching voraciously on something. A bit of string dangles from the corner of his mouth

Wolf Oooh, I'm so ravenous. All I've had to eat is one tiny little duckling … and of course that bag of sweeties. (*He turns defiantly to the audience*) Yes, I ate the whole lot of them, bag and all. (*He notices the string at the corner of his mouth*) Oh, I haven't quite finished the string from the bag, have I? (*He sucks it into his mouth like a piece of spaghetti*) But I'm still hungry. (*He moves threateningly towards the audience*) What I really need is a nice juicy, scrunchy, wriggling, resisting, screaming … human being.

The Fox enters

Fox   Look no further, evil beast.
                               I will arrange your human feast.
Wolf But the Boronskis have escaped and locked their doors.
Fox   Don't worry. Soon they will be in your jaws.

Music underscores her words

No. 10: So Alone
(*Singing*) They've done it once—they think they're
        awfully clever,
But no-one can escape the Fox for ever.
Stand still—and briefly from all thoughts abstain,
While I transfer my plan into your brain.

The Wolf freezes. The Fox makes a magic pass towards him and music indicates the passage of thought-waves between them. As the music stops, the Wolf jolts back to life, and a wolfish (inevitably, really) grin spreads across his features

Wolf It's brilliant! It's great! It cannot fail!
Fox   Of course not. In my Fox's magic tail
                               (*Singing*) I have more power, more cunning and
                                   more art
                               (*Spoken*) Than all the witches in the world. Depart!
                               (*Singing*) Shortly your main course I will serve,
                               But let Babushka act as your hors-d'oeuvre!

The Wolf hurries off, roaring and slavering in anticipation

                               And next I'll put Natasha in a trance.

"The Dance of Death"'s the measure she will dance!
But when she comes, she'll not see me—
Invisible is what I'll be.

She makes a magical gesture, as if cloaking herself. Then she makes another, as if drawing someone onstage

Natasha enters, looking sorry for herself

Natasha (*sighing*) Oh, life really is a mess.

She walks right past the Fox, who looks at her with evil intent

What's the use of being the daughter of Count Sergei Boronski if you haven't got any money? And now I'll probably never get to Moscow...

No. 10a: So Alone
I know I seem
So full of self-esteem—
But what I feel like
Nobody would dream.
Yes, I may look proud,
But under my shell
I'm the opposite extreme.

Deep down inside
I'm so dissatisfied,
Feeble, unsure and frightened...
Tho' those are the feelings I've been trying to hide.

They make me hide
The things I feel inside—
All of the hurt and anguish—
Though I know my pain will be mistaken for pride.

At the end of the song, the Fox is about to make another magic pass at her, when Ivan enters the opposite side of the stage, facing them. He carries a bag over his shoulder and his magic axe is glowing

He senses evil. Though he cannot see the Fox, he raises his magic axe in her direction

A shimmering glissando of music is heard, the Fox recoils angrily, and rushes offstage

Ivan (*coming forward to take Natasha in his arms*) It's all right, don't worry. It's gone.

Natasha (*finding she doesn't actually mind being in his arms*) I don't know what you're talking about, Ivan. What's gone? There was nobody here.

Ivan You must believe me, my lady. I am a man of honour.

Natasha Yes, that's true. (*Dreamily*) And a serf... (*Suddenly becoming aware of the situation and pulling herself away from him*) And a serf! What on earth do you think you're doing? I could have you horsewhipped for this.

Ivan (*drawing back respectfully*) I'm sorry, my lady. I was just trying to protect you.

Natasha Huh. I don't need protection.

Ivan You do, my lady. (*He indicates the bag*) And I have here some things that will help to keep you safe.

Natasha What are they? Where did you get them from?

Ivan They were given me by the old forester who was ... more than a father to me. I beg you to take them for your protection. (*Taking a small box out of his bag*) In this box is a powder which will make any person sneeze.

Natasha (*sarcastic*) Oh, very useful. Hay fever all the year round.

Ivan It is useful, believe me. Because so powerful is the sneezing this powder causes that it will immobilise even the strongest man. Take it.

Natasha (*putting it into her basket with a sigh of long-suffering*) Very well.

Ivan (*taking a stick out of his bag*) And this stick will defend its owner if he or she is attacked. (*He hands it to her*) All you have to do is say "Beat, beat, beat, beat, beat, little stick!"

Natasha Well, why doesn't it do it when you say that?

Ivan Because I have given it to you. I am no longer the stick's owner.

Natasha (*softening at his generosity*) Ivan, that's very kind. You know, you're the sort of man who... (*But she can't talk like this to a serf. Her old character reasserts itself*) Very well, I'll take these, if you insist. (*Moving off*) Now I must go.

Ivan My lady, will you allow me to accompany you to——

Natasha No!

Natasha marches off without even saying goodbye to him

Ivan Natasha...

But she has gone

One day. One day you will lose your pride, and airs and graces, and show your true character. And when the moment comes, I'll be ready. (*He goes into a wistful reprise of the chorus of the* Unrequited Love Duet)

No. 10b: Unrequited Love Duet (chorus reprise)
> Oh, my darling,
> Never fear—
> When you need me,
> (*Spoken*) I'll be here.

Sadly, Ivan goes offstage, in the opposite direction to Natasha

SCENE 11

Babushka's sitting-room

Babushka is in her mobile bed, knitting. She looks up to see the audience

Babushka Oh, hallo. All you serfs still out there, eh? Haven't had the interval yet, have you? No? I shouldn't think it'd be long now. Best to finish the first half on a nice high note, though, isn't it? And what higher note could there be than me singing a song for you? Can you imagine anything you'd enjoy more? (*Reacting to some imagined—or possibly real—response from the audience*) You didn't have to answer that. In fact, the song with which I am going to delight you and close the first half of this Siberian soap opera concerns my hobby. (*She pulls a length of her knitting out from under the covers. The knitting is in fact a very long multi-coloured scarf*) Knitting. So here it is—the first-half closer—my much-loved number which has been acclaimed in music halls all the way from the Volga to Vladivostok— *The Knitting Song!*

No. 11: The Knitting Song
> Oh, I'm a natty knitting nut from Nishni-Novgorod,
> And I'll be a nut for knitting till I die.
> But call me a knitting nit and it may hurt a bit...
> When you get a knitting needle in your eye.
>
> Now when I knit for profit I do frightfully well,
> And everything I knit is quickly bought.
> The money people pay is just ridiculous—
> Still, that is up to them, I would have thought.
> So when they ask the price,
> I multiply it twice...
> Then knit a natty number and add on another nought.

She pulls another length of knitting out from under the covers

Oh, I'm a natty knitting nut from Nishni-Novgorod,
And I'll be a nut for knitting till I die.
But call me a knitting nit and it may hurt a bit...
When you get a knitting needle in your eye.

She pulls the full length of the knitted scarf out from under the covers, and cheerfully tosses the end of it out through the open window

During the next verse, the Wolf appears at the window, pulling himself up on the end of the knitting

Then he pulls Babushka in her bed towards him

Now when I sing this song I always pride myself,
It doesn't sound as if it's learnt by rote.
No, each performance is a pure original
In which I let my hair down and emo-o-o-ote.
And, after my top C,
I sometimes change the key...
Then knit a natty number and attain a higher note.
Yes, I knit a natty number and attain a higher no...

By the end of the song, Babushka is right by the window, and the Wolf has his arms around her neck. Seeing what's happening, Babushka lets out a scream

Aargh!

Black-out

In the Black-out, there is heard a hideous crunching noise, then—after a little pause—a belch from the Wolf

The CURTAIN *falls*

Entr'acte

ACT II

SCENE 1

In front of the snow-covered forest cloth

The Fox enters triumphantly and sings

No. 12: Follow the Fox

Fox

My message is hatred, my meaning is harm
I trap and entrance by my terrible charm.
For any I choose I can have in my thrall,
Be here when I beckon, and come to my call.
By the glare of the sun or the gleam of the moon
I can make every one of them dance to my tune.

Enchanted and chained by my magical spell,
Now skidding, now sliding, now tumbling pell-
mell,
Led by delusion
O'er rivers and rocks,
In fear and confusion
They'll follow the Fox.
Follow the Fox,
Through fields of illusion
They'll follow the Fox.

Natasha enters, zombie-like, as if pulled on by the magic of the music and the force of the Fox's enchantment

During the ensuing verse and chorus, she does a kind of awkward dance, as if she has no control over her limbs, and her movements are all dictated by the Fox's magic string-pulling

(*Spoken*) I don't care for people—just human
detritus,
Prancing like puppets while I pull the strings,
And when I pull, they will dance like St Vitus,

Held without hope as the sorceress sings.

(*Singing*) I'll pull them, I'll push them, I'll send their
    limbs flying,
Till they're heavy and hurting and haggard and
    stressed;
But still they dance on till they think they are dying,
And, weary and wasted, they'll cry out for rest.
Their strength is so paltry they cannot prevail
Against all the power I have in my tail.

During the final chorus, the Fox circles round Natasha, brings her back to life and, slowly, with magical gestures, draws her offstage towards her doom

Bemused and bewitched by my magical brush,
The old ones, the new ones, will come in a rush,
Led by delusion
O'er rivers and rocks,
In fear and confusion
They'll follow the Fox.

Natasha has by now gone offstage to the horror that awaits her at Babushka's house. The Fox finishes the song on a note of triumph

Follow the Fox,
Through fields of illusion
They'll follow the Fox.

SCENE 2

Babushka's sitting-room

The setting is the classic one from the old fairy story. The Wolf is in the bed, dressed in Babushka's clothes. He holds a blanket up to hide his face, and slowly lowers it through the scene

Natasha enters through the front door, in her red riding hood and with the cloth-covered basket on her arm

The strains of an instrumental version of Follow the Fox *are heard. Natasha moves as if under strong enchantment, and the whole brief scene is played with a mythical, dreamlike quality. Natasha sits at the end of her grandmother's bed. She speaks in a distant, enchanted voice*

Natasha O Grandmother, what big eyes you have.
Wolf (*in a little old lady voice like Babushka's*) All the better to see you with, my dear.
Natasha O Grandmother, what big ears you have.
Wolf (*in a little old lady voice*) All the better to hear you with, my dear.
Natasha O Grandmother, what big teeth you have!
Wolf (*with a sudden roar, in his own voice*) All the better to eat you with, my dear!

The Lights suddenly dim, leaving only a reddish Light around the bed. The front of the bed opens up like an enormous car bonnet fringed with jagged teeth, from which more reddish light spreads. Natasha screams, as her silhouette is drawn into the gaping jaws

Black-out

SCENE 3

In front of the snow-covered forest cloth

The Fox enters, singing a reprise of Follow the Fox

No. 12a: Follow the Fox (reprise)
Fox   Follow the Fox, follow the Fox,
                            Through fields of illusion they'll
                            Follow the Fox.

As she sings, she lures on from offstage the zombie-like presences of Basil, Boris and Katerina. She leads them off to their doom

Ivan comes rushing onstage, holding up his axe, the head of which once again glows red

Ivan Don't worry, Natasha! I'll save you. I'm on my way.

Nobly, with his glowing axe held high, Ivan rushes offstage in pursuit of the others

SCENE 4

Babushka's sitting-room

The bed has disappeared, and the room looks ominously empty. The stove is out; no steam rises from the samovar

Katerina enters, followed by Basil and Boris

Katerina Mother. Mother, where are you?

Boris (*looking round*) She doesn't seem to be in this room.

Katerina (*sarcastically*) Sometimes you know, Boris, I am just struck dumb by the sheer, naked power of your intelligence.

Boris (*taking it as a genuine compliment*) Oh, thank you very much, Mummy.

Basil (*hugging himself*) Jolly cold in here, isn't it? Unlike Babushka to let the stove go out.

Katerina Maybe she's gone out for a walk with Natasha. Let's just see if they're coming along the path.

Katerina and her two sons move across to the front door and look out

While their backs are turned, the door on the other side of the stage opens and the Wolf peers out. He slavers and wipes his whiskers in anticipation of his next meal. He pops back inside the door before the others turn back

No sign. I hope they're all right...

Basil Oh, I'm sure they are.

Katerina Hm. Well, I'm just going to have a look if she's through in the other room. You two see if you can warm this place up a bit.

Katerina goes off through the door from which the Wolf peered out

Boris How do you think we can warm this place up then?

Basil (*moving across to look at the stove*) Well, I suppose the thing to do is get the stove lit.

Boris Yes, that's right. (*He calls off*) Olga! Masha! Irena! Could you come and light the stove?

Basil They're not here, you fool. This is Babushka's house.

Boris Oh yes, so it is. (*He moves across to the stove*)

Both brothers look dubiously at the stove

So looks like there's nothing we can do...

Basil No.

Boris Unless... I don't suppose... Basil, you don't think we could light the stove ourselves, do you?

Basil What? No, of course we couldn't. We're gentlemen. Gentlemen don't do anything useful.

Boris No. Sorry. Just a thought.

Basil Sometimes, you know, I despair of you, Boris.

From offstage is heard a roar from the Wolf, a little scream from Katerina, a crunching noise and, after a brief silence, a belch. Basil and Boris listen to these sounds in silence

Well, you might at least apologise.

Boris Mm? What for?

Basil Your tummy rumbling like that.

Boris It wasn't my tummy rumbling. It must have been your tummy rumbling.

Basil It jolly well wasn't!

Boris Well, it certainly wasn't mine. I say, I've just had a thought of how we could warm it up in here.

Basil (*without optimism*) How?

Boris We could do a dance. A Cossack dance. Gentlemen are allowed to dance, aren't they?

Basil Yes. Actually, that's a very good idea, Boris.

Boris Oh, thank you very much.

Basil Well, there has to be a first time for everything. All right, let's dance. Ah—one—two—three—and——

Cossack dance music and song starts. Basil and Boris go into a routine which involves much stamping, thigh-slapping, squatting on the haunches, putting their arms round each other's shoulders, and shouting "Oy!" The two brothers work together

No. 13: Cossack Dance

Boris ⎱ (*together*) Where is my vodka? Where is my glass?
Basil ⎰   Drink all you can pour,
                              Then a little more—
                              Fall on the grass!
                          Get up and then
                          Do it again—Oy!

Soon after the dance has started, the Wolf creeps onstage, and starts shadowing their movements

Basil goes into an elaborate solo routine with much whirling and kicking from a squatting position. Boris stands to one side watching this, clapping his hands to the rhythm. The Wolf stands beside him, and claps along. At first Boris does not seem to notice anything odd about this. Then he looks across at the person clapping alongside him. He gives the Wolf a cheery grin, and looks back at Basil. Boris does a double take and freezes. When he looks back, the Wolf's arms are out ready to trap him

The Wolf seizes Boris and carries him off into the other room

Basil finishes his solo routine with a triumphant "Oy!" From offstage is heard a roar from the Wolf, a little scream from Boris, a crunching noise and, after a brief silence, a belch

Basil You might at least say sorry this time.

The music reaches the cue for the double routine, and Basil goes back energetically into the dance

> Bring me more vodka. Pass it around.
> Drink all through the night,
> Get extremely tight—
> Fall on the ground!
> Get up and then—
> Do it again—Oy!

The Wolf enters, wiping his whiskers with relish

He moves alongside Basil, and joins in the song and dance, doing the exact movements that Boris had done previously, joining in the "Oy!"'s etc. They get into a position where they are dancing side by side with their arms across each other's shoulders. After a time Basil looks across to his partner. Initially he doesn't notice anything odd, then he does a double take and looks back in horror

The Wolf carries him offstage to the other room

The music continues as, from offstage is heard a roar from the Wolf, a little scream from Basil, a crunching noise and, after a brief silence, a belch

The Wolf comes in, again wiping his whiskers with relish, and energetically completes the song and dance

Wolf   Open more vodka. And then some more.

Drink the bottle dry,
Get extremely high
Fall on the floor!
Get up and then—
Do it again—Oy!

He finishes in a dramatic pose on the final "Oy!"

Black-out

Scene 5

In front of the snow-covered forest cloth

Ivan hurries on, still holding aloft his red-glowing axe

Suddenly the Light inside the axe goes off. Ivan stops and looks at it

In a puff of smoke, the Fox appears blocking his path

The Fox's words are underscored with music

Fox   See how your axe's magic drains away
                   When my far greater powers are brought in play.
Ivan You think that you'll defeat me, but you'll not.
Fox   Oh yes, I will. Now, Ivan, you have got
                   No magic, no Natasha, and no hope.
                   A lingering death is all your horoscope.
                   The Wolf has swallowed down Natasha,
                   Easy as a bacon rasher.
                   Next items in the wolf's cuisine are
                   Basil, Boris and Katerina.
                   Your fate is sealed, your race is run.
                   You are the loser and the Fox has won!
                   Your magic spells will prove of little worth
                   Against the greatest sorceress on earth.
                   And you're an adversary hardly worth the scorn
                   Of the most powerful creature ever born.
Ivan (*starting to lay a little plot*) Yes, I have been impressed by your powers,
     Fox, but I do think you're exaggerating a bit.
Fox   Exaggerating? What on earth d'you mean?
                   I am the greatest there has ever been.

Ivan All right, I admit you're quite good, but even you must recognize that
you're never going to be the absolute best.

The Fox looks at him, thunderstruck

I mean, so long as there's a greater magician with greater powers than
yours living only a few minutes walk from here...

Fox   Where? Show me the impostor and you'll see
                          I am much greater than he'll ever be.

Ivan Well, if you really want me to, I will. But I think you might regret it.
I mean, is it sensible for you to enter a contest in which you know you're
going to come out second best?

Fox   I never come out second. Quickly, Ivan, take
                          Me where this liar lives.

Ivan He's in the lake.

The cloth is drawn back to reveal the frozen lake set

SCENE 6

The frozen lake

*It is exactly as it was in Act I. The hole in the ice that Basil cut is still there.
Mist drifts across the scene. The action is continuous from the end of the
previous scene*

Fox   A fish? (*Scornfully*) Oh dear, you've really got me
                          scared.
                          A fish to take me on? Nobody's dared
                          For years to challenge my unrivalled force.
                          A fish? I'll serve him up with mushroom sauce.

Ivan This is no ordinary fish. It's the Giant Sturgeon. The old forester who
brought me up told me all about this creature's powers. It has control over
everything that moves by land or water. And it will remain in control of
everything until the moment that it's caught.

Fox   And by what method can the thing be caught?

Ivan It cannot be.

Fox   It can. I read your thought.
                          I know the forester taught you a charm
                          That can the Sturgeon's magic powers disarm.

No. 14: Frozen Lake

The Fox makes a magic pass at Ivan, who freezes

> (*Spoken*) You have no choice. You must do as I wish.
> Tell me the spell that will defeat this fish.

Ivan (*singing the charm like a zombie, as if he has no control of his actions*)
> "No baits or lures or fish-hooks will avail;
> No nets or traps will have the slightest worth.
> To catch the Sturgeon you will need the tail
> Of the most powerful creature on earth."

Fox
> Terrific! Great! Oh, this was meant to be!
> The Sturgeon's met his match and that is me.

Ivan (*coming out of his trance; spoken*) I didn't mean to tell you.

Fox (*spoken*)
> Well, you did!
> From my all-seeing eye no secrets can be hid.
> (*She moves to the edge of the hole and sits, with her tail dangling down into the water*)

> (*Singing*) My magic tail's the bait I must put down
> To catch this bold pretender to my crown.

Ivan (*self-mortifying*) Oh, I feel such a fool. Of all the information I could have given you, that spell is the one thing I should have kept hidden at all costs. The Giant Sturgeon is the only magician in the world whose power can challenge yours. If he's caught, there'll be no-one who can stop your regime of evil.

Fox (*singing*)
> Exactly. Now at last I hope it's plain
> That all resistance to my scheme's in vain.

Ivan (*moving towards the Fox and looking down at the hole in the ice*) Oh yes, definitely. I know now precisely how much power you have. (*He grins suddenly and changes tone to something more perky—even triumphant*) None. None at all.

The Fox looks at him aghast

> Go on, try to move.

The Fox strains, but is trapped by her tail in the ice

> I'm afraid you rather fell for that one, Fox. The water freezes very quickly

when the evening sets in. And of course, since all your magic's in your tail, your magic's frozen too.

Fox   How dare you! Why, you double-crossing cheat!

Ivan Takes one to know one, so that's very neat. Well, I suppose you'll just have to sit there until the ice thaws, won't you? Pity you've arranged for the winter never to end, isn't it?

He laughs and raises his axe, which again starts to glow with light

Ah, look, as your magic fades, so the power of my axe once again grows stronger. Right, I must go and rescue the Boronskis. You'd better stay there, Fox. Though, actually, I don't think you have much choice in the matter.

Ivan goes nobly off into the forest

The Fox tries again to move herself, but is locked in position. She snarls

Fox   You may have won this round, my handsome hero,
But in the long term view, your chance is zero.
I cannot move to stop you in your tracks,
But don't imagine that your magic axe
Can save you from my vengeance. Tit-for-tat's
Fair game. Come to your mistress, vampire bats!

No. 15: Vampire Dance

To suitable music, and with a sound of hideous squeaking, the vampire bats come flitting on to the frozen lake. They do a brief dance of obeisance to the Fox, ending in a tableau around her

(*Singing*) Go, my murky minions, go!
Neither love nor mercy show.
In your treatment of Ivan
Be as cruel as Genghis Khan.
Slowly, slowly, he must die.
Bite his veins and suck him dry!

With more hideous squeaking, the vampire bats flitter off the stage

The Fox is left looking rather pathetic in the middle of the frozen lake, as the Lights slowly go down

SCENE 7

In front of the snow-covered forest cloth

Ivan enters, pursued by the vampire bats, who surround him

The remainder of the scene is a choreographed fight (to music), which, after a couple of moments of danger (a cut to Ivan's throat and a bat briefly attaching itself), results in Ivan beating the bats off and continuing triumphantly on his way

SCENE 8

Inside the Wolf's stomach

The scenery is red, slimy and dangly, cluttered with lots of bits and pieces, remains of things the Wolf has eaten. Sound effects of nasty drippings, rumblings and gurglings are heard

Sitting on convenient organs are Katerina, Basil, Boris and Natasha. Their appearance is exactly as it was before they were eaten; Natasha still wears her red riding hood and carries her cloth-covered basket. They all look very disconsolate

Boris (*after a silence*) Perhaps we could sing a song to cheer ourselves up?
Natasha What kind of song?
Boris Well… One of those ones that are sung by the Volga boatmen.
Katerina I'm not having any Volga songs sung in my house, thank you very much.
Basil This isn't your house, Mummy. It's a wolf's stomach.
Katerina That may be so, Basil, but it's still no reason for a lady to lower her standards. (*She looks round testily*) Oh, what on earth's Mother doing?
Basil Just finishing her tour of the intestines.
Boris (*looking out over the auditorium*) I say! Look at all those serfs out there!

All four look out over the auditorium

Goodness, the wolf was hungry to eat all that lot.

Babushka emerges from the Wolf's entrails

There is a flubbery gastric sound

Babushka Oy, watch it, you cheeky gland! (*To the others*) Well, you have to admit—this animal's certainly got guts.

Katerina (*mournfully*) What do you mean?

Babushka Come on, do cheer up. That was a joke. A pretty offal one, I agree, but I do my best, according to my lights. Guts ... offal ... lights... Oh, for heaven's sake, make a bit of an effort.

Katerina Why?

Babushka Well ... because you've always got to look on the bright side.

Katerina Listen, Mother. My husband Sergei has been captured and enchanted, our fortune has been lost, I and the rest of my family are currently trapped inside the stomach of a ferocious wolf—in the company of a load of common serfs... Could you kindly show me the bright side I'm meant to be looking on?

Babushka Of course, Katya.

Katerina winces at the diminutive

There's always a bright side. (*She gestures round the Wolf's stomach*) I mean, look at this wonderful living environment in which we've found ourselves! It's great, isn't it?

Basil and Boris are not quite sure why they're agreeing but are caught up in Babushka's enthusiasm

Basil
Boris | (*together*) You bet!

Babushka leads into the song Interior Design, *showing the rest of the cast round in the manner of an estate agent showing off a house. The others quickly catch on to the idea, and join in with increasing vigour. They keep trying to get Katerina to sing too, but she resists until right at the end, when she joins in even more forcefully than the rest*

No. 16: Interior Design

Babushka (*spoken*)   Now just being here entitles
You to tour the creature's vitals,
With all features you can see in the brochure.
Though I do not wish to flatter me,
I'm an expert on anatomy,
And on body parts both well-known and obscure.
(*She gestures the others to sit down*)
So pull up a fleshy hummock
While we travel round his stomach

And I (*she sings*) hope you will enjoy the guided
tour…

	Tho' the light's a bit funereal,

Tho' the light's a bit funereal,
The heating is arterial,
And it's pumped around the building by the veins.

Basil   Tho' not well illuminated,
It's superbly insulated
And you'll be entirely damp-proof if it rains.

Boris   There's a Turkish generosity
In his Omental Tuberosity,

Natasha   Though his Dorsal Vertebrae look almost Greek

Basil   And there's something quite Norwegian
In his Epigastric Region…

Babushka   But the whole effect is wonderfully chic!

All (*except Katerina*)   Oh, the perfect home for me
Inside a wolf would be,
Where his nerves and veins and arteries entwine
It's the ultimate "des res"—
Or so the agent says—
And I long for such a dream home to be mine.
It's a marvel anatomical—
So well fitted, economical!
What a wonder of Interior Design!

Boris   And—oh!—that Gastric Follicle's
Both recherché and symbolical!
There's not a single feature been misplaced.

Natasha   As for Nodules—wish you'd seen 'em—
All around his Duodenum,
Where they say so much about the owner's taste!

Basil   There are extras and ancillaries
In his veins and his capillaries.

Boris   There's a very interesting three-piece suite.

Natasha   There's no flaw or no disfigurement—
A poem in every ligament—

Babushka   And the Waste Disposal Unit works a treat!

All (*except Katerina*)   Oh, the perfect home for me
Inside a wolf would be,
Where his nerves and veins and arteries entwine
It's the ultimate "des res"—
Or so the agent says—

And I long for such a dream home to be mine.
It's a marvel anatomical—
So well fitted, economical!
What a wonder of Interior Design!

Basil For this paradise abdominal
The rent is merely nominal.
You'll get a very favourable lease.

Boris Oh, that bit there at the end, it's
Just his Vermiform Appendix,
Which does nothing—just a conversation piece.

Natasha All the colour's done so cunningly—
And that Spleen has come up stunningly!
While his Colon's the divinest thing of all!

Katerina (*finally succumbing to pressure from the others, and joining in with great energy; speaking*) If you like that, perhaps you'll
Love his Super-renal Capsule.
As for (*she sings*) Bladders—I'm surprised he's got the Gall!

All (*including Katerina*) Oh, the perfect home for me
Inside a wolf would be,
Where his nerves and veins and arteries entwine
It's the ultimate "des res"—
Or so the agent says—
And I long for such a dream home to be mine.
It's a marvel anatomical—
So well fitted, economical!
What a wonder of Interior Design!

They finish in a tableau. Then Katerina moves away, in a huff again

Babushka Come on, Katya. We got you singing in the end. Surely that's cheered you up.

Katerina No, it hasn't. Nothing's going to cheer me up except some really good news.

Babushka Well, I've got some good news for you. When I was exploring the wolf's intestines, I met someone who was thought to have been lost for ever.

Katerina (*sounding hopeful*) Oh, really?

Babushka (*gesturing offstage*) Yes—and here he is! You can come in now.

Katerina (*moving excitedly towards the entrance*) Sergei! My husband!

But no. Instead, onstage comes the Wolf's first victim—the smallest duckling. It preens its feathers nervously

(*Disappointed*) Oh.

Babushka See. If this poor little thing can be saved, then so can we.

Katerina "Saved" is a relative term, Mother. Yes, the duckling's alive ... just as we are—but we're all still stuck inside this wolf's stomach! And has anyone got any idea of how we're going to get out?

They all look glum and shake their heads. Then the smallest duckling tiptoes across to Babushka and quacks softly in her ear

Babushka Hey, that's terrific. Well done. The duckling says that, being covered with feathers, he knows how much feathers can tickle people's throats and make them cough ... and he's suggesting that if we all tickle the wolf's insides ... then he might cough us all out.

Katerina It'd never work. There aren't enough of us to make any difference in this huge stomach. He wouldn't feel a thing.

Babushka He would if we got all the serfs to help us too. (*She looks out over the auditorium*) Do you think the serfs would help us?

Basil After the way Mummy's talked about them, I would think it's very unlikely.

Natasha Unless we could find some way of bribing them with something.

Babushka Well, do you know... I might have just the thing for that. (*Moving to the entrance to the intestines*) In my tour of the wolf's intestines... (*She reaches offstage to produce the bag of sweeties*) ...I found this. And I was thinking, if the serfs help us make the wolf cough ... we could reward them with these sweeties. (*To the audience*) Do you think that's a good idea, serfs?

The audience, hopefully: "Yes!", "You bet!", etc.

Basil How exactly are we going to get them to help us?

Babushka Oh, that's easy. We'll get them to sing *The Tickling Song*. All together now—one—two—three—and...

They all go into singing The Tickling Song. *After a few lines, Babushka silences them*

No. 17: The Tickling Song

All
    To beat the Wolf and see him off,
    We'll tickle his tum and make him cough.
    And, if we do, there is no doubt
    His coughs will send us flying out...

Babushka (*to the audience*) Oy, why are you lot not singing?
Natasha They don't know the words.
Babushka That's true. They don't.
Basil How can we teach them?
Babushka It's all right. In my tour of the intestines, I came across just the thing. A nice cake the wolf had eaten. Go on, boys, it's over there. I think it could be just the thing for us.

Boris and Basil go offstage and return with a cut-out cake, which opens like a birthday card to reveal that it has the words of The Tickling Song *written inside it*

There—now isn't that convenient? All right, no excuses now. Let's all do *The Tickling Song*—and you all follow the movements that we do too— all right?

Babushka and the rest of the cast take the audience through the song, which goes as follows

All   To beat the Wolf and see him off,
                                 We'll tickle his tum and make him cough.
                                 And, if we do, there is no doubt
                                 His coughs will send us flying out.
                                 So all cheer up and don't be glum—
                                 And tickle and tickle and tickle his tum!

There are simple movements throughout the song, and on the last line, all the cast—and, hopefully, the audience too—reach up and make tickling movements with their fingers

                                 To beat the Wolf and see him off,
                                 We'll tickle his tum and make him cough.
                                 And, if we do, there is no doubt
                                 His coughs will send us flying out.
                                 So all cheer up and don't be glum—
                                 And tickle and tickle and tickle his tum!

After the audience instruction, the cast do as much of the traditional dividing the audience in two, dividing it by gender, etc. to sing the song as is thought appropriate

                                 (*With the audience*) To beat the Wolf and see him
                                       off,

We'll tickle his tum and make him cough.
And, if we do, there is no doubt
His coughs will send us flying out.
So all cheer up and don't be glum—
And tickle and tickle and tickle his tum!

At the end Babushka calms everyone down

Babushka Well, that was very good. Very good indeed. Basil and Boris, do you think they were good enough to be rewarded by sweeties?

Basil and Boris reach a decision after a pause

Basil ⎱ *(together; uncertain)* We-ell…
Boris ⎰
Babushka Oh, I think they were. Don't you really?
Basil ⎱ *(together)* Yes.
Boris ⎰
Babushka All right. Let's throw some sweeties out to them, shall we?

Babushka, Basil and Boris go into the sweetie-throwing routine. As the euphoria subsides, they return to the action of the pantomime

Well, that was fun, wasn't it?
Katerina Fun it may have been, Mother, but there's one thing I can't help noticing.
Babushka What's that then, Katya?
Katerina It didn't work.
Babushka What?
Katerina We're still in here, aren't we?
Babushka Oh yes. Yes, so we are. (*She turns to the audience*) Excuse me, could we have our sweeties back, please? You've had them under false pretences.
Katerina It's hopeless. We'll be trapped in here for ever by the fox's magic.
Natasha (*suddenly having an idea*) Then we must counter it with other magic. (*She indicates her basket*) Ivan gave me these magic gifts.
Katerina I don't like you having anything to do with Ivan, Natasha. You weren't brought up to mix with woodcutters.
Natasha He's a good man, Mummy. Only now, stuck down here, am I beginning to realize just how good a man he is. (*A little pang*) I wish he were here. I can't bear the thought that I'll never see him again.
Babushka You'll have time enough for all that mushy stuff, Natasha. What magic gifts did Ivan give you?

Natasha Look. (*She lifts the cloth on her basket*) He gave me a magic stick...
(*She takes out the box of powder*) ... and I've got this magic powder.
Babushka What does it do?
Natasha It makes you sneeze. And the sneezing is so powerful that it will
immobilise even the strongest man.
Babushka (*taking the box from her*) Well, that's great. If we can't make the
wolf cough us all out, then we'll jolly well make him sneeze us all out! (*She
opens the box and takes out a handful of the glittery powder. She scatters
it into the auditorium*)

*They all wait in silence. Then the sound effect of the build-up to the most
enormous sneeze in the world is heard. As it reaches its crescendo, the cast
all do a unison double take of amazement, as if the audience have suddenly
disappeared*

Basil Good heavens!
Boris Where've all the serfs gone?
Babushka It's worked! He's sneezed them all out! Come on, us next. You
go first, Katya.
Katerina What?
Babushka Come on. Stand here. (*She gestures her daughter to stand on the
edge of the stage*)

Katerina does as she's told

Hold on to everything ... because here you go! (*She scatters more glitter
over the edge of the stage*)

*As the build-up to a second sneeze begins, the Lights dim. Caught in a
spotlight, Katerina whirls round and round to the sound of the second sneeze.
While she is doing this, the sides of the Wolf's stomach open out in a
"transformation" effect. While Katerina continues to spin, the snow-covered
forest cloth is drawn across, so that only Katerina is in front of it, still spinning
around*

SCENE 9

In front of the snow-covered forest cloth

*As the sneeze dies away, the Lights come up, and Katerina comes to an untidy
halt on the edge of the stage. She looks curiously at the audience*

Katerina Oh, there you are, serfs. (*She adjusts her hair*) That kind of transport plays havoc with one's hair-style. (*She smiles ingratiatingly at the audience*) Don't you find that?

Another giant sneeze is heard. Katerina cowers away from it

> *Then Babushka and the smallest duckling come spinning across from the wings, as if projected by the Wolf's sneeze. They clatter into Katerina, sending her flying*

They all pick themselves up

Babushka (*to the duckling*) There. You're free. Now you fly straight back home to your mother.

> *The duckling flutters off*

Katerina I wasn't expecting you to be the next one out.
Babushka Boris wanted to have a go with the sneezing powder, so I let him.
Katerina Oh, I hope he doesn't do anything wrong with it.
Babushka You don't need to worry. What can he do wrong? Only an idiot could make a mess of making the wolf sneeze.
Katerina That's why I'm worried. We are talking about Boris, after all.

> *Another, shorter sneeze sends Basil spinning across the stage. He clatters into Katerina and Babushka, sending them flying*

They pick themselves up

Babushka Look. Even Boris can't go wrong with this.

> *Another, even shorter, sneeze, and Boris comes spinning across the stage. He is carrying the box of powder. He clatters into the others, sending them flying*

They pick themselves up

See? No problem.
Katerina (*pointing suspiciously to the box*) What's that, Boris?
Boris It's the sneezing powder, Mummy. The powder that's got us all out of the wolf's tummy.
Katerina All?

Boris nods complacently

Where's Natasha, Boris?

Boris (*turning round to look for his sister*) Well she must be... (*He realizes the full import of what's happened, puts his hand to his mouth and lets out a little gulp*) Erm...

Katerina You idiot, Boris! Just wait till I get you home! (*She moves forward, as if to strike him*)

Boris turns tail and runs off, hotly pursued by Katerina, Babushka and Basil

Black-out—or, if preferred, a chase round the auditorium!

SCENE 10

The Boronskis' sitting room

The room is still in a state of winter neglect and decay

The Wolf enters, hungry and furious. He roars at the audience

Wolf I need more human flesh! I'm ravenous! My belly's empty! (*He takes in the audience*) Ooh, there are some nice, juicy serfs out there, aren't there? I'll come and eat some of you!

But before the Wolf can leap down into the auditorium, Boris rushes on upstage, still pursued by Katerina, Babushka and Basil. They do not see the Wolf at the edge of the stage

Katerina You stupid boy, Boris! Just let me get my hands on you!

Boris I'm sorry, Mummy. I'm really sorry! (*He bangs into a chair, which stops him short*)

Basil and Babushka grab hold of him and bend him over the chair, as Katerina starts spanking him. The Wolf advances towards them

Wolf How nice of you all to drop in for dinner.

They turn, aghast, to face him

I think I've eaten you lot before, haven't I? I don't normally like meals repeating on me... but in this case I'm prepared to make an exception. (*He laughs cruelly*) You are all about to die!

They cower as the Wolf advances on them menacingly

Then Ivan enters with his axe held aloft

Ivan No, Wolf! You are the one about to die. I am Ivan, and my magic axe will bring your reign of terror to an end!

With an evil laugh, the Wolf turns to face his adversary

Wolf I have waited for this moment, Ivan. Only one of us can survive this encounter and it's not going to be you!

Ivan We'll see about that, Wolf. On my side, I have a magic axe, the strength of my own body, and a pure heart!

Wolf And on my side, Woodcutter, I have all the mighty power of undiluted evil!

While the Boronskis cower and cheer on Ivan, he and the Wolf fight (with music underscoring their actions in silent-movie style). It is a to-and-fro contest, now one with the upper hand, now the other. Ivan's axe swishes close to the Wolf's head; the Wolf's claws only just miss Ivan's flesh. Then Ivan begins to get the upper hand. He forces the Wolf back, till the beast stumbles and lies unprotected on the ground. The Boronskis cheer, as Ivan raises his axe for the coup de grâce

I wouldn't do that, Ivan.

Ivan I can think of no possible reason why I shouldn't.

Wolf Because, if you do so, you run the risk of injuring the woman you love. Natasha is still in my belly!

Ivan (*taken aback*) What? But surely she... (*Taken off his guard, he looks over to see if Natasha is with the rest of her family*)

The Wolf seizes his opportunity, kicks upwards at Ivan's midriff, and sends the woodcutter hurtling across the stage. The axe flies from Ivan's hand. With an evil laugh, the Wolf picks it up and advances menacingly on his fallen enemy

Wolf The situation's rather different now, isn't it, Ivan? (*He raises the axe above his victim*) A brave try, but I'm afraid your life is about to end.

Ivan I'm not afraid to die. And, Natasha, know that, even in death, I will always love you!

Natasha's Voice (*heard on strange subterranean echo*) And I will always love you too, Ivan.

Wolf (*looking down at his stomach with amazement*) Good heavens, it must have been someone I've eaten.

Ivan tries to take advantage of the diversion, but the Wolf is too quick for him. The beast puts his foot on Ivan's chest, and once again raises the axe high

Nothing can save you now, Ivan!

Natasha's Voice (*heard on strange subterranean echo*) Beat, beat, beat, beat, beat, little stick!

A strong drumbeat is heard—also on strange subterranean echo—and the Wolf starts to leap about in the manner of a wolf who is being beaten internally in his stomach by a magic stick

Babushka It's the magic stick!

Ivan seizes his chance; he manages to roll free and wrest the axe from the Wolf's hand

Ivan Now we will see who is the stronger, Wolf!

The Boronskis cheer, as Ivan, with mighty strokes of his axe, forces the Wolf—still suffering from abdominal beating—to back away from him

With Ivan in the ascendant, the two of them disappear offstage

The Boronskis move to watch and give a commentary on the action

Basil Oh, nice hit, Ivan!

Boris He's got the wolf down!

Babushka (*bellowing like a woman at a wrestling match*) Go on, my son! Knock his blooming block off!

Katerina Really, Mother. I wish you wouldn't talk like that.

Babushka Oh, shut up, you silly little snob! Let yourself go for once. (*She calls offstage*) Bash the living daylights out of him, Ivan!

Katerina (*getting caught up in the excitement of the moment and becoming dead common*) Yes, Ivan, have the rotter's guts for garters!

Babushka looks with amusement at her daughter

(*Looking a little sheepish for a second, then bawling out*) Go on, nail the swine, Ivan!

Babushka That's better, Katya. (*She calls offstage*) Murder him!

Basil Ivan has overpowered the wolf!

Boris (*covering his eyes*) Ooh, I don't want to look. Is he going to cut the wolf open with his axe to free Natasha?

Basil No—he's using his hunting knife.

A howl is heard from the Wolf offstage

Babushka Oh, neat as an imperial surgeon. Look at it—just like filleting a fish.
Katerina Natasha!

Natasha comes rushing onstage, and into her mother's arms. In the way of fairy stories, incidentally, she shows no marks from the impromptu Caesarean which has just delivered her. She still wears her red riding hood

Natasha Mother!
Katerina Oh, my darling, it's so good to see you!

Natasha turns to look offstage

Ivan enters

They look at each other for a moment, then rush into each other's arms

Ivan Natasha!
Natasha Ivan!
Ivan I knew, if I waited long enough, you would come to love me.
Natasha I've been a fool. Why did it take me so long?
Katerina (*drawing Natasha to one side*) Erm… Natasha dear. This is all very delightful, and I can understand you getting carried away in the emotion of the moment, but I would like to point out that Ivan is still just a humble woodcutter.
Natasha (*rushing back to Ivan*) I couldn't care less.
Katerina (*miffed*) Oh dear. I do sometimes worry about the way I brought up my children, you know.
Natasha (*ignoring her mother*) I couldn't care less, because, whatever you do, you're still you, Ivan—and it's you that I love!

Katerina shakes her head in disbelief that she's actually hearing this

Ivan And, through all your arrogance and airs and graces, it's you that I love, Natasha.
Natasha I'll stop being like that, Ivan, I promise—when I'm with you.

No. 18: Requited Love Duet
Ivan   Through the dangers and the threat

Of magic and of crime,
I always knew my love for you
Would stand the test of time.
Through reverses and regret,
I somehow always knew
When danger passed, why, then at last
You'd feel my way too.

Natasha   I'm all confused, I'm all upset,
I've had a change of heart,
And now I cannot face the thought
That we should ever part.
Forgive my pride. I'll be your bride.
Then you and I'd agree
Our strife is past, our love will last
As long as you and me.

Both   I don't want
Natasha   To be without you
Ivan   A life with you
Natasha   Is my ideal.
Ivan   Until you want me
Natasha   To marry you?
Ivan   And love me too.
Both   Here's what I feel—
Oh, my darling,
Natasha   I know my mind—
Ivan   Never fear—
Natasha   I know I love you.
Ivan   When you need me,
Natasha   Choose your own kind,
Ivan   I'll be there.
Both   Not far above you.

At the end of the song, the lovers go into a clinch

Then the Wolf staggers onstage, clutching at his wounded stomach. He keeps his back to the audience because—for reasons that will soon become apparent—he is not in fact the actor playing the Wolf, but an S.M. in the Wolf's skin. (Alternatively—and more dramatically effectively—the Wolf has a loose-fitting suit, which he can actually remove onstage)

Ivan sees the Wolf, picks up his axe and moves towards the beast with homicidal intent. He raises his axe, as if about to despatch his adversary

Ivan And now, Wolf, your evil reign is about to end!

But Natasha steps between her lover and his victim

Natasha No, Ivan.
Ivan But, Natasha, this beast has terrorised every member of your family.
He is entirely evil.
Natasha No, no-one is entirely evil—except perhaps the Fox. This is now
just a feeble, wounded beast. Let him stagger off into the forest to lick his
wounds.
Ivan But he abused the power and strength that he was given. And now I have
the power to punish him for that.
Natasha (*softly*) But you have the greater power to forgive him.

*Ivan thinks about this for a moment, then slowly lowers his axe. Natasha goes
forward to the Wolf*

Leave us now. Go back to the distant forest where you came from—and
mend your ways.

*She leans forward to plant a little kiss on the top of the Wolf's head. There
is a sudden flash of lightning and an enormous puff of smoke. When it clears,
the Wolf has vanished, and in his place stands a handsome middle-aged man
in aristocratic dress. (This effect can either be achieved by the S.M./Wolf
going offstage and being replaced by Sergei or—much more dramatically—
by Sergei actually removing his Wolf costume when screened by the smoke.
Which course is taken will obviously depend on the inventiveness of the
wardrobe mistress.) Ivan and the Boronskis react with astonishment to the
apparition of Sergei*

Father!
Katerina (*rushing into his arms*) Sergei!
Boris ⎫
           ⎬ (*together, coming forward to greet him*) I say! Daddy!
Basil ⎭
Katerina But, my love, what on earth happened to you?
Natasha Were you the wolf all the time?
Sergei Yes. I was the victim of another of the Fox's spells. She turned me
into that evil monster. I was powerless against her magic. But you have
saved me, Natasha.
Natasha How, by kissing you?
Sergei Yes. Your goodness overcame the Fox's evil.
Babushka Well, well, well, here's a turn-up. Any other spells we're going
to find suddenly undone?

Sergei There is one more.

Babushka What's that? Are you going to tell me that the Fox enchanted me too? She hid me in the body of an ancient grandmother, but in fact I am really a ravishing young twenty-year-old?

Sergei No. Sorry, mother-in-law, not that.

Babushka Just as well, really. I have enough difficulty fighting the men off as it is.

Sergei No, the other spell the Fox told me about was one she made many years ago. Do you remember the story that was going round about the Tsar's baby son having been stolen from his cradle?

Babushka Yes, of course.

Sergei Well, it was true. The Fox herself stole the baby. She left it in the forest to be eaten by wild beasts, but fortunately the baby was found...

Ivan By an old forester?

Sergei By an old forester. (*He goes down on his knees to Ivan*) God bless you, your Royal Highness. You are the son and heir of the Tsar of All the Russias.

The rest of the Boronskis all go down on their knees to Ivan

Ivan Please. I do not want anyone to kneel to me. Whatever my title, I am still just another human being. Stand.

They do

Katerina I always said he seemed a cut above the average woodcutter, didn't I?

Boris No, you didn't, you fibber. You always said——

Sergei Silence! We'll have no squabbling now that I've returned. The Boronskis are going to be a united family again—and we are all going to work together for the common good.

Katerina By the common good, Sergei, I assume you mean the good of ... our sort of people?

Sergei No, Katya. I mean that we are all going to work together for the good of the serfs.

Katerina What a peculiar idea.

Sergei Come on, Boronskis, we must start to prepare a great celebration...

Katerina Well, surely, we just give orders to the servants. (*She calls offstage*) Olga! Masha! Irena!

Sergei No, Katya, we're going to do this ourselves.

Katerina What? Us? The Boronskis? Actually do something?

Sergei Oh yes. Everything's going to be very different in this family from now on.

Katerina (*faintly*) Oh dear.

Sergei And the boys are going to help too.

Basil ⎫
Boris ⎭ (*together; faintly*) Oh dear.

Natasha There is one thing...

Sergei What?

Natasha (*turning to Ivan*) Ivan, when you were just a humble woodcutter and I was the daughter of a Count, you wanted to marry me... But now I'm still only the daughter of a Count, and you are the son and heir to the Tsar of All the Russias, who could marry a princess from any of the royal families of Europe... Are you sure that hasn't made you change your mind?

There is a silence, while all the characters focus on Ivan. Then he shakes his head

Ivan No, Natasha. You are the only woman I have ever wanted. And if I were Emperor of the Universe, you would still be the one I want.

The rest of the cast cheer, as the lovers go into each other's arms. Then Babushka tries to attract everyone's attention

Babushka Listen! Listen! Be quiet, all of you! Listen!

They are silent. The sound of a bird singing is heard. It is joined by other birds, whose music melts into the introduction to the Winter's Ending, Spring is Coming *song*

Basil! Boris! Open the shutters!

Basil and Boris do as they are told. Sunlight spills in through the open windows. Green shoots can be seen outside

The fox's spell is ended! Spring is here!

Sergei Come on! Let the children join our celebration!

The children who played the ducks and vampire bats come on dressed as Russian peasants, and join the song and dance

Let's sing!

No. 19: Winter's Ending, Spring is Coming

All   We're the Boronskis, now we are back

To the station in life where we should be,
We're top of the tree and ahead of the pack,
And our lives are as nice as they could be
From the Black Sea to Siberia,
There is no-one our superior

Sergei   But pride can come before a fall!
Katerina
Natasha ⎫ (*together; piously*) We've found that life's a college,
Boris   ⎬   Where we all have learnt … self-knowledge.
Basil   ⎭
Babushka (*spoken*)   Oh yes? And I'm the Sultan of Bengal!
Sergei (*calling out*)   Come on! Let the children join our chorus!

The children, dressed in Russian peasant style, come on and do a folk dance, while they all sing the chorus

All   Winter's ending, spring is coming,
Soon the ice will start to thaw
Green will show
Up through the snow,
And the melting water pour
Down the gutters.
Open shutters
Will let sunshine through your——

The song is interrupted, and a chill cast over the proceedings, by the entrance upstage of—the Fox

Fox (*stalking downstage*) Stop! Don't imagine that evil can be defeated for ever. I am still alive and still determined to ruin your happiness!

Sergei But your magic is defeated. Your power has gone.

Ivan You no longer even speak in rhyme.

Fox My power will return. I'll make your lives a misery. I'll live to plague you all again!

She turns on her heel to stalk majestically upstage. But by turning, she reveals that her magnificent tail is no longer there. The assembled characters laugh at the sight

(*Turning on them in seething fury*) You may laugh now, but you will not always be laughing. So the only way I could escape the ice was to leave my tail in the lake. But my magic powers will come back. If you think you can destroy evil for good…

The following two lines are underscored with music

> (*Singing*) Despair, such hopes will always be in vain
> My magic tail will grow—and I'll be back again!

There is a puff of smoke and the Fox vanishes

There is a brief, uncomfortable moment, then the assembled throng revert to their song and dance. They start very tentatively, but soon are back on full throttle

No. 20: Winter's Ending, Spring is Coming (Finale)

All	We're the Boronskis, now we're restored
	Back to our pride and possessions.
Sergei	But don't be afraid, though. We've taken on board
	In the future we must make concessions.
Natasha	And so, by way of penance,
	We'll be kinder to our tenants,
Katerina	And realize that serfs are human too.
Basil	We'll be more democratic
Boris	And less aristocratic.
Babushka (*spoken*)	Believe that … well, it's up to you!

All	Winter's ending, spring is coming,
	Soon the ice will start to thaw.
	Green will show
	Up through the snow,
	And the melting water pour
	Down the gutters.
	Open shutters
	Will let sunshine through your door.

The cast finish the song in a tableau, and go into their curtain calls routine. If a final rousing chorus is needed, they sing the following reprise of Interior Design

No. 21: Calls and Interior Design (reprise)

> Now, the perfect ending song—
> We're back where we belong,
> And our future's looking blissful and benign
> Now we never want to roam
> Or leave the family home,
> 'Cos to stay here evermore will suit us fine.

Though the perils were precipitous,
Still, the ending's serendipitous—
What a perfect piece of Pantomime Design!

CURTAIN

FURNITURE AND PROPERTY LIST

Further dressing may be added at the director's discretion

ACT I

SCENE 1

On stage: Furniture for the **Boronskis'** sitting-room, including a stove and a samovar
Large leather bag with drawstring mouth containing sweeties

Off stage: Bunch of snowdrops (**Natasha**)

Personal: **Natasha:** warm knitted red riding hood

SCENE 2

On stage: Snow-covered forest cloth

SCENE 3

On stage: **Boronskis'** sitting-room
Cups of tea
Novel

SCENE 4

On stage: Snow-covered forest cloth

Off stage: Bag of sweeties (**Wolf**)

SCENE 5

On stage: **Babushka's** sitting-room
Large stove
Dress

Off stage: Bed on wheels with false body, large piece of knitting
               (**Babushka**)
            Pile of logs (**Ivan**)
            Bag of sweeties (**Wolf**)

Personal: **Ivan:** axe in leather holder on his belt

SCENE 6

On stage: Snow-covered forest cloth

Off stage: Small pie (**Fox**)

SCENE 7

On stage: **Boronskis'** sitting-room
            Snow dusted over stove and furniture
            Novel
            Chair
            Red riding hood

Off stage: Wood (**Ivan**)
            Basket with white cloth over it (**Katerina**)

Personal: **Ivan:** book of spells, axe

SCENE 8

On stage: **Katerina's** bedroom cloth

SCENE 9

On stage: Frozen lake set
            Skateboard disguised as large disc of ice

Off stage: Handful of feathers (**SM**)
            Large rod (**Boris**)
            Fishing bags containing large saw, hammer, chisel, tin of
               worms (**Basil**)

SCENE 10

On stage: Snow-covered forest cloth

Off stage:	Axe, bag containing small box and magic stick (**Ivan**) Basket (**Natasha**)
Personal:	**Wolf:** bit of string in mouth

SCENE 11

On stage:	**Babushka**'s sitting room Mobile bed Knitting—very long multi-coloured scarf

ACT II

SCENE 1

On stage:	Snow-covered forest cloth

SCENE 2

On stage:	**Babushka**'s sitting-room Trick "bed"
Off stage:	Cloth-covered basket (**Natasha**)

SCENE 3

On stage:	Snow-covered forest cloth
Off stage:	Axe (**Ivan**)

SCENE 4

On stage:	**Babushka**'s sitting-room
Strike:	Bed

SCENE 5

On stage:	Snow-covered forest cloth
Off stage:	Axe (**Ivan**)

SCENE 6

On stage: Frozen lake set

SCENE 7

On stage: Snow-covered forest cloth

SCENE 8

On stage: **Wolf**'s stomach
Lots of "internal" bits and pieces
Remains of things **Wolf** has eaten
Organs

Off stage: Cloth-covered basket (**Natasha**)
Bag of sweeties (**Babushka**)
Cut-out cake, like birthday card with *The Tickling Song* written
on it (**Boris** and **Basil**)
Box of glittery powder (**Natasha**)

SCENE 9

On stage: Snow-covered forest cloth

Off stage: Box of powder (**Boris**)

SCENE 10

On stage: **Boronskis'** sitting room

Off stage: Axe (**Ivan**)

LIGHTING PLOT

Practical fittings required: 2 coal stoves, glowing magical axe
Various interior and exterior settings

ACT I, Scene 1

To open: Semi-darkness, hot coals glow through grille of stove

Cue 1   A door is suddenly opened on one side of the stage   (Page 1)
             Sunlight through door

Cue 2   **Natasha** throws back the shutters   (Page 1)
             Sunlight through window

ACT I, Scene 2

To open: Overall general lighting

No cues

ACT I, Scene 3

To open: Hot coals glow through grille of stove

Cue 3   **Fox**: "And I condemn you to eternal cold!"   (Page 9)
             Change lighting to harsher, colder glare

Cue 4   Second magical chord   (Page 10)
             Cut glow from stove

Cue 5   Shutters and windows blow open   (Page 10)
             Effect of gust of snow blowing in

ACT I, SCENE 4

To open: Overall general lighting

No cues

ACT I, SCENE 5

To open: Overall general lighting, glow from stove (optional)

No cues

ACT I, SCENE 6

To open: Overall general lighting

No cues

ACT I, SCENE 7

To open: Lighting suggests a desolate air

No cues

ACT I, SCENE 8

To open: Overall general lighting

No cues

ACT I, SCENE 9

To open: Lighting to heighten icy beauty of the lake

Cue 6   All rush off in horror   (Page 34)
           Black-out

ACT I, Scene 10

To open: Overall general lighting

*No cue*s

ACT I, Scene 11

To open: Overall general lighting

Cue 7   **Babushka** screams   (Page 39)
             Black-out

ACT II, Scene 1

To open: Overall general lighting

*No cue*s

ACT II, Scene 2

To open: Overall general lighting

Cue 8   **Wolf**: "All the better to eat you with, my dear!"   (Page 42)
             Fade lights down quickly, leaving only reddish light
                around bed

Cue 9   Jaws open from front of bed   (Page 42)
             Increase the spread of reddish light

Cue 10   **Natasha** screams, drawn into gaping jaws   (Page 42)
             Black-out

ACT II, Scene 3

To open: Overall general lighting

*No cue*s

ACT II, SCENE 4

To open: Overall general lighting

Cue 11   **Wolf** finishes in a dramatic pose   (Page 46)
           Black-out

ACT II, SCENE 5

To open: Overall general lighting

*No cue*s

ACT II, SCENE 6

To open: Frozen lake lighting

Cue 12   **Fox** is left alone   (Page 49)
           Slowly fade lights down

ACT II, SCENE 7

To open: Overall general lighting

*No cue*s

ACT II, SCENE 8

To open: Gloomy interior

Cue 13   Second sneeze sound effect begins   (Page 57)
           Fade lights down, bring up spot on **Katerina**

ACT II, SCENE 9

To open: Overall general lighting

Cue 14   The sneeze sound effect dies away   (Page 57)
           Bring up overall lighting, fade spot on **Katerina**

Cue 15   **Katerina, Babushka** and **Basil** exit   (Page 59)
             Black-out

ACT II, Scene 10

To open: Lighting suggests desolate air

Cue 16   **Natasha** kisses **Wolf**   (Page 64)
             Flash of lightning

Cue 17   **Basil** and **Boris** open the shutters   (Page 66)
             Bring up sunlight through open windows

EFFECTS PLOT

ACT I

Cue 13	**Basil**: "Boris, where are you?" *Crash offstage*	(Page 30)
Cue 14	**Basil** attaches worm to hook *Crash offstage*	(Page 30)
Cue 15	Black-out *Hideous crunching noise—and belch*	(Page 39)

ACT II

Cue 16	**Katerina** screams offstage *Crunching noise, silence, belch*	(Page 44)
Cue 17	**Boris** screams offstage *Crunching noise, silence, belch*	(Page 45)
Cue 18	**Basil** screams offstage *Crunching noise, silence, belch*	(Page 45)
Cue 19	As **Fox** enters *Puff of smoke*	(Page 46)
Cue 20	To open Scene 6 *Drifting mist*	(Page 47)
Cue 21	**Vampire Bats** enter *Hideous squeaking*	(Page 49)
Cue 22	**Vampire Bats** exit *More hideous squeaking*	(Page 49)
Cue 23	To open Scene 8 *Effects of nasty drippings, rumblings and gurglings*	(Page 50)
Cue 24	**Babushka** enters *Flubbery gastric sound*	(Page 50)
Cue 25	**All** wait in silence *Build-up to enormous sneeze*	(Page 57)
Cue 26	**Babushka** scatters more glitter *Build-up to enormous sneeze*	(Page 57)

Cue 27   To open Scene 9   (Page 57)
             Fade sneeze

Cue 28   **Katerina**: "Don't you find that?"   (Page 58)
             Another giant sneeze

Cue 29   **Katerina**: "We are talking about Boris, after all."   (Page 58)
             Another, shorter sneeze

Cue 30   **Babushka**: "Even Boris can't go wrong with this."   (Page 58)
             Another, even shorter, sneeze

Cue 31   **Ivan**: "I will always love you!"   (Page 60)
             Natasha's Voice *on strange subterranean echo as*
                  page 60

Cue 32   **Wolf**: "Nothing can save you now, Ivan!"   (Page 61)
             Natasha's Voice *on strange subterranean echo as*
                  page 61 with drumbeat

Cue 33   **Natasha** kisses **Wolf**   (Page 64)
             Enormous puff of smoke

Cue 34   **All** are silent   (Page 66)
             Birdsong, joined by other birds, melting with music

Cue 35   **Fox**: "…and I'll be back again!"   (Page 68)
             Puff of smoke